Monograph Series of the
Carnegie Endowment for International Peace,
Division of International Law
No. 1

THE SOURCES OF MODERN
INTERNATIONAL LAW

BY

GEORGE A. FINCH

*Assistant Director, Division of International Law,
Carnegie Endowment for International Peace;
Secretary, American Society of International Law; Managing Editor, American Journal of International Law;
Member of the Bar of the District of Columbia*

WASHINGTON
CARNEGIE ENDOWMENT FOR INTERNATIONAL PEACE
700 JACKSON PLACE, N.W.
1937

COPYRIGHT 1937
BY THE
CARNEGIE ENDOWMENT FOR INTERNATIONAL PEACE

PRINTED IN THE UNITED STATES OF AMERICA
AT THE RUMFORD PRESS, CONCORD, N. H.

FOREWORD

A few years ago—in 1932, to be specific—the Carnegie Endowment for International Peace had the happy idea, as it turned out, of establishing at the University of Michigan at Ann Arbor a summer session for the teaching of international law. The successive sessions, held with the coöperation of university authorities, were open to teachers of international law and international relations in the American colleges, in order that they might learn both by precept and by example, as it were. That is to say, it was hoped that they would profit not only from the substance of the lectures but also from observing the various methods of presentation of the different phases of international law laid before them by the respective lecturers.

The professors—perhaps it would be better to say instructors—conducting the summer term are five in number, and in the past five years there has been but a single change, although the student body, comprising not more than forty nor less than thirty, has changed from year to year. In the first year the instructors, in alphabetical order, were Messrs. Dickinson, Finch, Reeves, Scott, and Wilson. In the second year, however, Professor Dickinson was called to the University of California, where he is at the present day Dean of the Law School of the University. He was succeeded by Professor Charles Cheney Hyde, and this year Mr. Hyde will be succeeded by Professor Percy E. Corbett of McGill University in the Dominion of Canada.

The course which Mr. Finch chose, and which he has presented with modifications from year to year, dealt with "The Sources of Modern International Law." This comprised six lectures, which were open to discussion by the student body, as were all the other courses. The volume which now makes its appearance contains the six lectures, somewhat enlarged and arranged under chapter heads.

Mr. Finch's lectures have been of great interest and importance to the student body of the summer sessions at Ann Arbor. But they have also been highly appreciated elsewhere, for upon invitation of the Curatorium they were delivered in French, in the summer of 1935, at the *Académie de Droit International établie avec le concours de la Dotation Carnegie pour la Paix Internationale*, and they appear in the official publication of the Academy, the *Recueil des Cours*, which is on the shelf of every ministry of foreign affairs. Mr. Finch has now allowed himself to be persuaded to issue them in English in such form that a student of international law who has not been privileged to attend his courses at Ann Arbor or is unable to read them in the French version may now have an English copy at his or her elbow.

The lectures are as follows: "Factors which have Contributed to the Growth of International Law"; "Natural Law as a Source of International Law"; "Modern Text-Writers on International Law"; "Custom as a Source of International Law"; "Treaties as a Source of International Law"; and "International Law in the Courts."

That the published lectures will be of great value is evident from the fact that for some thirty years Mr. Finch has been accumulating a fund of both practical and theoretical knowledge of his subject-matter. This knowledge he has acquired not only through much investigation and study but also through association with the Department of State, the Carnegie Endowment's Division of International Law, and such organizations as the American Society of International Law, of which he is Secretary and of whose *American Journal of International Law* he is Managing Editor. Therefore his knowledge of international law is practical as well as theoretical; for he has been not only a witness to its growth but has taken part in its development. His aim and purposes are set forth in his Introduction to the present volume, which is destined to enjoy a widespread appreciation not only by his former auditors in the New and in the Old World but by all of those who have at heart the development and universal acceptance of the law of nations.

After an intimate association and collaboration with Mr. Finch of over thirty years—to be precise, thirty-one years to the day—I unreservedly recommend the volume, slender in form but closely knit, and predict that it will become the *vade mecum* not merely of those who are beginning their studies of international law but also of those who are privileged to profess and to practise it.

JAMES BROWN SCOTT,
Director of the Division of International Law

Washington, D. C.,
  April 1, 1937.

PREFACE

In the Foreword which Dr. Scott has done me the honor to prefix to this monograph—my first presumption to expound international law beyond the limits of occasional articles and editorial comments in the *American Journal of International Law*—he has stated the circumstances which gave occasion for the preparation of the notes from which the lectures have been prepared. The content of these chapters, as Dr. Scott also indicates, shows some results of years of thinking about international law from the points of view of many writers, of differing nationalities, whose contributions to the science the author has read in editing some thirty volumes of the *American Journal of International Law*.

The Summer Sessions at Ann Arbor provided the opportunity to present the material in the form in which it is now made public. The method of presentation was chosen after careful consideration of the needs of mature students whose training in the elements of international law may not have been sufficiently thorough to provide an adequate background for the teaching of advanced courses. It was also adopted in the hope of provoking, among writers and teachers addicted to a certain "school" of international law, more catholic thinking in a subject which is universal in its extent and affects all peoples and governments, whatever their condition or characteristics, and whether they be at peace or war. A science affecting the destiny of the whole human race cannot be properly developed from particularistic or nationalistic embryos. It needs to be studied as a biological science in the laboratory of the world's experience. In the following pages the surface only has been scratched in such an ambitious design.

GEORGE A. FINCH

Washington, D. C.,
April 6, 1937.

CONTENTS

	PAGE
INTRODUCTION	I

CHAPTER I

FACTORS WHICH HAVE CONTRIBUTED TO THE GROWTH OF INTERNATIONAL LAW ... 3

CHAPTER II

NATURAL LAW AS A SOURCE OF INTERNATIONAL LAW ... 15

CHAPTER III

MODERN TEXT-WRITERS ON INTERNATIONAL LAW ... 30

CHAPTER IV

CUSTOM AS A SOURCE OF INTERNATIONAL LAW ... 44

CHAPTER V

TREATIES AS A SOURCE OF INTERNATIONAL LAW ... 59

CHAPTER VI

INTERNATIONAL LAW IN THE COURTS ... 76
    Prize Courts ... 76
    National Courts ... 80
    International Tribunals ... 90

BIBLIOGRAPHY ... 100
INDEX ... 117

THE SOURCES OF MODERN INTERNATIONAL LAW

INTRODUCTION

In the introduction to his treatise on *International Law* published in 1905–6, the late Professor Lassa Oppenheim, of Cambridge University, who described his treatise as a work "for students written by a teacher," made this statement: "Many years of teaching have confirmed me in the conviction that those who approach the study of international law should at the outset be brought face to face with its complicated problems, and should at once acquire a thorough understanding of the wide scope of the subject." A few years later a professor of law of Harvard University, who also lectured in Columbia University, wrote that "on no subject of human interest, except theology, has there been so much loose writing and nebulous speculation as on international law." [1] Without concurring in such a general denunciation of the literature of international law, it may be acknowledged that writers readily admit the existence of much confusion, especially in the study of the sources of international law. For example, the French writer Pradier-Fodéré, over half a century ago, complained that "authors do not agree either upon the classification or the respective importance of the sources of international law, and they do not even appear to possess a clear idea of the signification of the word source. Generally they confuse sources with the foundation of international law, and sometimes they consider as a source of that law what is only the intellectual instrument by means of which its rules are discovered." [2] Some years later, Professor J. de Louter, of the University of Utrecht, urged the importance of the study of the sources of international law because, he said, "nowhere is the confusion greater and hence nowhere is clearness more necessary than here." [3] A recent Canadian writer, Professor Percy E. Corbett, of McGill University, writing on the subject of "The Consent of States and the Sources of the Law of Nations," states that "we need examine only a very small number of the general works on the law of nations to realize that 'source' is used by different writers, sometimes by the same writer at different times, to express the concepts of cause, origin, basis and evidence." Professor Corbett offered his own definition of these terms as follows:

1. The cause of international law is the desire of states to have the mutual relations which their social nature renders indispensable regulated with the greatest possible rationality and uniformity.

2. The basis of international law as a system and of the rules of which it is composed is the consent of states.

[1] John C. Gray, *The Nature and Sources of the Law* (1909), p. 122.
[2] Translation from *Traité de droit international public*, Vol. I (1885), p. 78.
[3] Translation from *Droit international public positif* (1920), Vol. I, p. 42.

3. The origins of the rules of international law, which may also be called "the sources" of that law—though the word "source" has such a history of confusion behind it that it might well be abandoned—are the opinions, decisions or acts constituting the starting-point from which their more or less gradual establishment can be traced.

4. The records or evidence of international law are the documents or acts proving the consent of states to its rules. Among such records or evidence, treaties and practice play an essential part, though recourse must also be had to unilateral declarations, instructions to diplomatic agents, laws and ordinances and, in a lesser degree, to the writings of authoritative jurists. Custom is merely that general practice which affords conclusive proof of a rule.[1]

From these comments and criticisms it is evident that any definitions of the sources of international law which may be offered will be accepted or rejected according to the point of view from which they are formulated and the agreement or disagreement of the reader with that point of view. The Positivist, who bases the system of international law entirely upon the consent of states, will certainly not agree as to the source of that system with the Naturalist, who sees international law existing above and beyond the purview of the individual states subject to it. Neither will the Naturalist agree on this question with the Positivist; and the same disagreements will appear in degree between the several intermediate schools of thought as to the nature of international law. Professor de Louter helped to clear up some of the reason for the confusion which exists when he pointed out that the study of the sources of international law "is closely related to the conception of the nature of international law in general," for, he explained, "that conception is faithfully reflected in the choice of the sources from which one considers that it may be deduced." [2]

As it is not the purpose in this place to dogmatize upon the nature of international law and certainly not to add to the confusion of thought already existing on the subject of the sources of international law, no new definition of terms will be attempted. Prudence suggests that we follow the lead of one who has labored long and fruitfully in the field of international law and whose authority is world-wide. The Honorable John Bassett Moore, in the introduction to his new monumental series entitled *International Adjudications*, declines to take part in this very discussion between the writers. His attitude is stated as follows:

Being desirous to deal with the substance of things, and, by avoiding as far as possible wars of epithets, to save a great cause from needless injury and attrition, I have placed the words "source" and "evidence" in the alternative, thus leaving to their partisans, who may often agree except in terminology, the unchallenged enjoyment of the title they prefer.[3]

[1] *British Year Book of International Law* (1925), pp. 29–30.
[2] *Op. cit.*, p. 42.   [3] Vol. I, p. lxxviii.

CHAPTER I

FACTORS WHICH HAVE CONTRIBUTED TO THE GROWTH OF INTERNATIONAL LAW

Generally speaking, international law in the meaning of the term as used in modern times, did not exist during antiquity and the first part of the Middle Ages. It was born of necessity after a number of separate and independent states had successfully established themselves in propinquity one with another. According to Hallam, "the law of nations was first taught in Germany, and grew out of the public law of the empire,"[1] which "was composed of no less than three hundred and fifty-five different sovereign states, of various descriptions, feudal, ecclesiastical, and municipal, of unequal extent and relative importance."[2]

The modern international community of states, based upon the ideas of territorial sovereignty, nationality, and the legal equality of states, is generally regarded as dating from the Treaties of Westphalia of 1648, which ended the Thirty Years' War and sanctioned, with some adjustments, the constitution of the Germanic Empire and established the modern European States System on a conventional basis. The English term "International Law" itself was not used until another century and a half when it was coined by the English jurist, Jeremy Bentham.[3]

But the relations of sovereign nations with one another, and especially the intercourse between their respective nationals, have been affected in many ways by circumstances which antedate the relatively short period of three hundred years that the Family of Nations, as it is known today, has been in existence. From these antecedent circumstances certain factors appear to have exerted an influence on the growth and development of the principles of modern international law. Whether they be called "origins" or "sources" is unimportant to this discussion. Perhaps a better word might be the "roots" from which important branches of the science as we now know it have grown. These factors, recognized by and collected from a number of authorities, may be given as follows:

1.—*The spread of Roman law through Western Europe beginning with the twelfth century.* According to Oppenheim, the "Civilians main-

---

[1] *The Middle Ages* (1893), Vol. I, p. 576.
[2] Wheaton, *History of the Law of Nations* (1845), p. 72.
[3] *Great Jurists of the World* (1914), p. 541. See Bentham's *Principles of International Law,* 1786–1789, published in *The Works of Jeremy Bentham* (1843), Vol. II, p. 535.

tained that Roman law was the law of the civilized world *ipso facto*
through the emperors of the Germans being the successors of the emperors of Rome.   Their commentaries to the *Corpus Juris Civilis* touch
upon many questions of the future international law which they discuss
from the basis of Roman law.   The Canonists, on the other hand,
whose influence was unshaken till the time of the Reformation, treated
from a moral and ecclesiastical point of view many questions of the
future international law concerning war." [1]   To the same effect is Sir
Henry Sumner Maine, who, lecturing before the University of Cambridge in 1887, said: "A great part of international law is Roman law,
spread over Europe by a process exceedingly like that which, a few
centuries earlier, had caused other portions of Roman law to filter into
the interstices of every European legal system." [2]

2.—*The revival of trade and commerce during the Middle Ages.*   At
first regarded as contraband, trade with foreign merchants was generally forbidden except for a limited period at fairs usually held at the
time of Church festivals.   These fairs rapidly developed in popularity
as sources of profit for the traders and of revenue to the feudal lords or
kings who quickly saw the advantage of granting fair franchises.
For several centuries these great fairs were the chief means of international commerce in Western Europe.   But to travel alone and un-
protected at that time was to invite attack and plunder, so for self-
protection the merchants attending the fairs travelled in company and
at first provided for their own defense.   Later, it became the custom to
purchase safe-conduct from the chiefs and lords of the countries through
which the caravans passed.   The peace of the fair constituted the great
and outstanding essential to its success, for without the assurance of
safe-conduct and safe residence merchants would not have found it
worth their while to risk their lives and property in foreign travel, and
without these fairs the increasing needs of the international exchange of
commodities could not have been supplied.   Gradually the peace of the
feudal lord was superseded by the peace of the king, and sometimes by
the peace of God imposed by the Church.   The influence of the Church
also made itself felt in enlarging the scope of the rights of foreigners
attending the fairs by enforcing good faith and loyalty in the dealings
between those in attendance.[3]   The part that these fairs played in the
formation of modern public law is thus described by M. Huvelin:

The influence of the fairs on our public law, on the movement of municipal
emancipation and on the enfranchisement of the commons is undeniable.   More
striking still is their influence on the relations of international law; the term

---

[1] *International Law* (2d ed.), Vol. I, p. 55.
[2] *The Whewell Lectures on International Law* (2d ed.), p. 20.
[3] Summarized largely from the work of Wyndham A. Bewes, entitled *The Romance of the Law Merchant* (1923).

"fair" is the equivalent of the term "peace." The reaction against the principles of primitive hostility is working under the influence of commercial needs. If, perhaps, it is incorrect to say that the relations of hospitality, containing the germ of the most characteristic institutions of international law, are only born of the necessities of trade, it must still be recognized that they have powerfully contributed to second in this matter the affinities of religions and races. Thanks to the progress of the peace of the fairs and their safe-conducts, the communications of foreigner with foreigner become more certain; international relations multiply; transactions are surrounded by guaranties; and the ideas of good faith and of the loyalty which should preside over commerce are more and more developed. At the same time the means of transport are being perfected. Men, hitherto thrown back upon themselves in the bosom of a family group, assume contact with each other; original mistrust is weakening; and already there appear tendencies to sociability which hitherto nothing had revealed. Little by little the last vestiges of primitive hostility disappear. Reprisals and the *droit d'aubaine* cease. Privileges which had for long made fairs and markets asylums withdrawn from the common law, gain more and more ground. The peace of commerce conquers the world, and fairs only disappear after accomplishing their work.[1]

3.—*The formation of leagues of trading towns for the protection of their trade and citizens engaged in trade.* These leagues stipulated for arbitration of controversies, acquired trading privileges in foreign states, and waged war when necessary to protect their interests. The most celebrated was the Hanseatic League, consisting of the free cities of Bremen, Hamburg, Lübeck, and others of North Germany, which was formed in the thirteenth century and lasted until 1630, when its last general Diet was held at Lubeck.[2] In the course of the century following the establishment of the Hanseatic League about 1260, it extended to upwards of eighty cities whose great depots at Bruges, London, Bergen, and Novgorod spread a trading network throughout all the lands of the North. The League of the Rhine (about 1250) and the Swabian League (about 1376) linked the Baltic Confederacy with the Mediterranean merchants. At Bruges, at London, and in the Italian cities the woolen manufactures of Flanders were exchanged for the wines of Southern France and the silks of Sicily and Greece; at Novgorod and Constantinople the western dealers met the vendors of furs and spices from the distant East.[3]

4.—*The development of maritime law which was made necessary by the spread of international trade on the sea.* The rules and customs of this trade were collected into written codes. The first of these was probably the Rhodian Sea Laws, a very old collection of maritime laws put together between the sixth and the eighth centuries. Then came the maritime laws of the town of Amalfi, in Italy, the collection of which,

---

[1] *Essai historique sur le droit des marchés et des foires* (1897), pp. 594–5.
[2] Phillimore, *Commentaries upon International Law* (3d ed.), Vol. I, p. 111.
[3] Walker, *History of the Law of Nations* (1899), Vol. I, p. 117.

known as the Tables of Amalfi, dates at the latest from the tenth century. This compilation, with such additions as were necessary, was the source of the famous *Consolato del Mare*, which the Venetians adopted as their maritime code in 1255, and which was later accepted by other maritime peoples. Transplanted to France and to the shores of the Baltic, the rules of the *Consolato* furnished the foundation for the judgments of Oléron, a twelfth century collection of the decisions of the maritime court of Oléron, France, and for the later fourteenth century collection of the maritime laws of Wisby. "The *Consolato del Mare*," says Dr. Thomas A. Walker, "was accepted by all the chief traders of the Mediterranean northern seaboard. Originating in the practice of merchants and seamen, sanctioned by gradually extending usage, and dealing with the mutual rights under the various chances of maritime adventure of owners and freighters, masters and mariners, with pilots and deserters, with jettison and collisions, loss by pirates, by the detention of princes, and by the act of God, these codes at once set out a veritable common law of the sea and furnish an eminently instructive illustration of the method of evolution of all international law."[1] To it may be traced the sources of the modern law of prize. The *Consolato* also recognized the institution of consuls in the character of magistrates who accompanied vessels upon their voyages, which was probably general as early as 1279.

In this connection, mention must also be made of the part played in the development of modern international law by the great overseas companies organized in the maritime countries of the sixteenth and seventeenth centuries. The formation of these companies was the result, at first, of efforts to improve the economic position of the home country and the financial condition of the government by opening up new trade routes with distant countries. Larger ships were needed, the sums of money required were beyond the capacity of single traders to provide, and the perils and risks were greater than in the trade with neighboring peoples. The traders consequently associated themselves in joint stock companies organized under governmental encouragement. These companies later became not only the means of increasing commerce with distant countries but of colonizing newly discovered lands.[2] The history and activities of such European companies as those which traded with the East and West Indies, in the South Seas, and with other parts of the New World are too well known to need any detailed description. It will suffice for our present purposes to call attention to the fact that the contest between the Dutch and Portuguese over rights of navigation and commerce in the East Indies was the *raison d'être* for

---

[1] Walker, *op. cit.*, Vol. I, pp. 116–17. See also Wheaton, *op. cit.*, p. 66.
[2] G. N. Clark, *The Seventeenth Century* (1929), Chap. III.

the work on the *Mare Liberum* by Hugo Grotius, who had been retained
by the Dutch East India Company to justify the capture by one of its
ships of a Portuguese galleon in the Straits of Malacca in the year 1602.
His dissertation, in which he defended the right of the Dutch to take
part in the East India trade, was published in 1609 and has become a
source book on the modern law of the freedom of the seas.[1]

5.—*The growing custom on the part of states to send and receive permanent legations.* We are indebted to the late Dr. David Jayne Hill[2] for
a most interesting account of the history and establishment of this system of intercourse between states. "Even among the most barbaric
nations," he says, "the inviolability of envoys appears to have been
recognized from very early times; . . . the ceremonies of reception at
the Gothic court of Theodoric," who ruled Rome under the title of consul shortly before the year 500 A.D., "were in imitation of those customary at Byzantium, where great pomp and elaborate formality were
in vogue. . . . Even the Frankish and the Visigothic kings endeavored
to reproduce the etiquette of Constantinople." Five hundred years
later, "the West was still in the crude beginnings of courtly etiquette,"
Dr. Hill continues, "but the East had long been habituated to a studied
courtesy, and it was from its more polished manners that Western
Europe was later to acquire those polite forms of intercourse which were
to mark the age of chivalry." The Papacy long employed occasional
legates, "while Constantinople, without organizing permanent missions,
had a large experience in diplomatic intercourse. Foreign princes,
particularly in the Orient, were always desirous of relations with the
Eastern Empire, and ambassadors were constantly received and sent."
Dr. Hill states that "the Byzantine diplomacy was not only admirably
organized, but presided over by a department of foreign affairs long before this office was established anywhere else in Europe. A fixed cere-
monial had gradually grown up, whose formulas were considered of
great importance." It was from contact with the East that Venice acquired that schooling in diplomacy which the Italians organized into an
elaborate system, and later communicated to the rest of Europe, thus
furnishing the basis of our modern diplomatic practice.[3]

Dr. Hill places the date of the birth of the modern diplomatic system
at the beginning of the sixteenth century. He says: "Among the results of the rivalry for supremacy in Italy, the most important and the
most enduring was the establishment of permanent diplomatic rela-

---

[1] The discovery in 1864 of Grotius' manuscript entitled *De Jure Praedae*, written in
1604–1605, shows that the *Mare Liberum* constituted Chapter XII of that treatise.
See introductory note by James Brown Scott, and the authorities there cited, to the
English translation of *Mare Liberum*, entitled *The Freedom of the Seas*, by Ralph van
Deman Magoffin, published by the Carnegie Endowment for International Peace in
1916.
[2] *A History of European Diplomacy*, Vol. I (1911), pp. 36–41. [3] *Ibid.*, pp. 206–9.

tions between the chief European countries." As already pointed out, the occasional sending and receiving of embassies had always been customary, but Dr. Hill states that "the continuous residence of diplomatic agents in foreign capitals was unknown until the affairs of Italy rendered it imperative." The wars of Italy, he says, awakened the monarchs of Europe to the necessity of constant vigilance and associated action and of the need and value of alliances between the powers. It was in close connection with the great coalitions which followed that the institution of permanent diplomatic representation was developed during the reigns of Louis XII, Ferdinand the Catholic, and the Emperor Maximilian. Thus came into being the *Corps diplomatique*, the first permanent international representation of sovereign states. As to the original nature and functions of this *Corps*, and of the possibilities of its development, Dr. Hill writes:

Without organization and possessing no code except its own usages, which gradually took the form of customary law, the diplomatic body was an aggregation of living molecules without vital relations and without a soul. Questions of form, ceremony, and precedence quite inevitably became the chief objects of its interest, until a later age gave its existence a new significance through the regulation of its functions by principles of jurisprudence and conventional agreement. Had this body been from the first an association of authorized agents for the maintenance of international justice and equity, the history of Europe might have been altogether different; but the political theory of that time made no provision for a rule of law among the nations.[1]

As a consequence of the permanent residence of foreign envoys, questions concerning their position in the countries of residence had to be considered, and thus gradually grew up the international rules concerning the inviolability and exterritoriality of diplomatic agents.

6.—*The establishment of permanent standing armies.* An important factor in the growth of the modern law of war was the practice of great states, dating from the fifteenth century and developed during the Thirty Years' War, of maintaining permanent standing armies. Medieval warfare had been largely conducted by hired mercenaries normally engaged for a campaign and paid off at the end of it. Their commanders were contractors who undertook to supply a certain number of troops in exchange for a certain sum of money, and the obedience of the men was rendered primarily to their employer, the commander.[2] In some cases these hired armies were supplemented by national defensive armies, or so-called militia, unworthy of the name of disciplined troops. "The feudal levies were without coherence and seriously deficient in organization and discipline; they lived on the country in which they fought, or through which they passed . . . and spared neither neutral nor enemy in their exactions in the way of food, forage

[1] *A History of European Diplomacy*, Vol. I, pp. 207–8.   [2] Clark, *op. cit.*, p. 103.

and shelter. . . . They lived from hand to mouth, and maintained no magazines or stores of food for use in future operations." When supplies were available for issue to prisoners of war, they were usually held for ransom; when such supplies were not available, prisoners were often put to the sword.[1]

During the whole course of the seventeenth century, it has been calculated that there were no more than four complete calendar years of general peace in Europe. "War, therefore, may be said to have been as much a normal state of European life as peace, and the history of armies was one of the hinges on which the fate of Europe turned."[2] Armies not only increased in size, but their relation to the state changed, as well as their organization and the art of war, especially after gunpowder began to be used. Statesmen began to see that it would be more efficient and more economical to keep troops through the winter instead of paying them off and starting their campaign with fresh and probably untrained troops. The princes engaged in the Thirty Years' War one after another began to keep standing armies and by the time of the wars of Louis XIV it was normal for a sovereign to have an army in time of peace.[3]

The supply of mass-armies became a problem too big for private enterprise and the state had to take over this, as it took over the rest of the control of armies. To keep up the great arsenals and magazines of food, which the large scale of warfare made necessary, the states became great buyers, and this was one of the controlling causes of change in the organization of industry and commerce. State control meant great changes in both the armies and states. In some cases the army organization became the nucleus of the central government, and the general development of European institutions was greatly influenced by the fact that large standing armies, made efficient under state management and control, became instruments upon which the states could rely to carry out their policies.[4] Strict discipline was necessary for the training and morale of standing armies, and its imposition by the state favored the rise of general rules and more humane practices of warfare.

7.—*The Renaissance and the Reformation as factors in the development of modern international law.* According to Oppenheim, "the Renaissance of science and art in the fifteenth century, together with the resurrection of the knowledge of antiquity, revived the philosophical and aesthetical ideals of Greek life and transferred them to modern life. Through their influence the spirit of the Christian religion took precedence of its letter. The conviction awoke everywhere that the principles of Christianity ought to unite the Christian world more than

[1] Gen. G. B. Davis, "The Prisoner of War," *American Journal of International Law,* Vol. 7 (1913), p. 525.
[2] Clark, *op. cit.,* p. 98.   [3] *Ibid.*   [4] *Ibid.,* pp. 101–8.

they had done hitherto, and that these principles ought to be observed in matters international as much as in matters national." But, he states, "the Reformation put an end to the spiritual mastership of the Pope over the civilized world. Protestant States could not recognize the claim of the Pope to arbitrate as of right in their conflicts either between one another or between themselves and Catholic States."[1]

8.—*Plans for maintaining international peace.* The revival of the feeling of Christian solidarity was expressed especially in the form of proposals for establishing and maintaining peace among the peoples of Christendom. As early as 1306 Pierre Dubois proposed an alliance between all Christian powers for the purpose of maintaining peace by the establishment of a permanent court of arbitration to settle differences between the members of the alliance.[2] A century and a half later, in 1461, Podiebrad, King of Bohemia, negotiated with other courts for the foundation of a Federal State to consist of the existing Christian states with a permanent congress of ministers.[3] A plan which made a nearer approach to practical politics, was the so-called Grand Design of Henry IV of France, revealed in the memoirs of his Minister Sully. Henry, whose immediate object was to reduce the House of Austria, proposed to divide the whole of Europe proportionately between fifteen powers in such a way as to leave no cause for envy on the ground of equality and nothing to fear on the ground of the balance of power. Three religions, the Catholic, the Lutheran, and the Calvinist, were to be formally recognized, and disputes which might arise were to be settled by a General Council of Representatives modelled after the Amphictyonic Council of ancient Greece. The Treaty of Alliance and League between Henry IV and Queen Elizabeth, signed at The Hague on October 31, 1596, appears to have envisaged the calling of a general congress to bring the league into existence during the year 1597, but the death of the Queen in 1603 and the subsequent assassination of Henry in 1610 ended the project.[4]

The most celebrated unofficial peace plan of this period was *Le Nouveau Cynée* by Eméric Crucé, which appeared in 1623. The French author of this book undertook to counsel the princes of Europe of his day somewhat in the same fashion that Cyneas, a favorite of Pyrrhus, counselled the King of Epirus three centuries before Christ. Crucé urged the war lords of Europe to cultivate peace, to eschew war, and to settle their controversies by arbitration. He was a seventeenth

---

[1] *International Law* (2d ed.), Vol. I, p. 57.

[2] *De Recuperatione Terre Sancte.* See Schücking, *Die Organisation der Welt* (1909), pp. 28–30, and Vesnitch, "*Deux précurseurs français du pacifisme*" (1911), pp. 24–50.

[3] Darby, "The Bohemian Project," Grotius Society, Transactions, Vol. 4, pp. 170–9, 195–8.

[4] See Darby, *International Tribunals* (1904), p. 10 for text and p. 16 for comment on the Grand Design of Henry IV.

century apostle of the doctrine of the good neighbor in international relations. He proposed a universal union that should include not only Europe but all the world, the finest fruit of which, he said, would be the encouragement of commerce. He advised the monarchs to make provision so that their subjects might traffic without fear both by sea as well as by land, to facilitate means of communication, to encourage the practical arts of industry and the study of the sciences.[1]

Other schemes of this character that deserve to be mentioned are:

De Monarchia of Dante, the great Italian poet, written about 1309, but not published until 1559. Dante's thesis was "that each nation develop its peculiar genius to the fullest extent, and in order to be able to do this, let each nation become a member of a World-State, under the guidance of a Central Court of Justice that will regulate international affairs." This essay has been said to be "the first powerful reasoned legal argument in Europe, based on premises that are irrefutable and eternally true, in defense of international government." [2]

The European Diet, Parliament or Estates, published in 1693–1694 by William Penn, the English Quaker missionary and founder of the colony, now the state, of Pennsylvania in the United States. Penn proposed the creation of a sovereign deliberative body to meet at regular intervals where the sovereigns of Europe might establish rules of justice for their mutual intercourse as well as settle all differences between them that could not be adjusted by diplomatic means. The decisions of this tribunal were to be enforced, if necessary, by all the other sovereigns members of the Diet.[3]

The Project for Perpetual Peace of the Abbé Saint-Pierre, circulated anonymously during the Congress at Utrecht (1712–1713), at which the author was present as a French secretary, and later published over his name in Paris in 1716. This project was an elaboration of the Grand Design of Henry IV. An interesting feature of the project was the provision for the establishment in different towns of chambers for maintaining commerce, and each sovereign was to "lend his hand to the execution of the judgments of the chambers of commerce, as if they were his own judgments." The project also provided that the European union for peace should endeavor to procure the establishment of a similar union in Asia.[4]

Cardinal Alberoni's Scheme "for reducing the Turkish Empire to the obedience of Christian princes, and for a partition of the conquest, to-

---

[1] The plan of Emeric Crucé, published at Paris in 1623, is reprinted in the original French and in English translation in Darby, *International Tribunals*, p. 22. See also *The New Cyneas of Emeric Crucé*, edited with an introduction and translated into English from the text of 1623 by Thomas Willing Balch (Philadelphia, 1909).

[2] *Leagues of Nations, Ancient, Mediæval and Modern*, by Elizabeth York (1919), Chap. II, pp. 68–9.

[3] Darby, *ibid.*, pp. 56–63.   [4] Darby, *ibid.*, pp. 70–97.

gether with a scheme of perpetual diet for establishing the publick tranquility." This scheme was published at London in English in 1736, the translation having been made from the Italian manuscript in the hands of the Sicilian Ambassador at the court of France.[1]

The Perpetual Peace of Immanuel Kant, the philosopher of Königsberg, published in 1795. Kant contended that peace is the final goal of international law, and he proposed to preserve international peace by forming a voluntary, permanent congress of nations with which every neighboring state might be invited to associate itself. "It is only in this way," he argues, "that the idea can be realized of establishing a public law of nations which may determine their differences by a civil method, like the judicial proceedings among individuals, and not by a barbarous one (after the manner of savages), that is to say, by war." [2]

An Essay on a Congress of Nations for the adjustment of international disputes without resort to arms, by William Ladd, President of the American Peace Society, published in 1840. The essay provided for a congress of nations to consider and establish principles of international law, which were to be embodied in treaties; and also to form a court of nations to take cognizance of such cases as might be freely referred to it but whose decisions should be merely advisory.[3]

Other peace plans there were, too numerous to mention here, which may be studied especially in the literature on international organization.[4] They are all Utopian, some more so than others. They vary in terms from generation to generation according to the conditions prevailing and the international political problems to be met at the time each was proposed. As to their importance in the development of international law and organization, Oppenheim makes the following comment:

> They preached again and again the gospel of the organization of the Family of Nations, and although their ideal has not been and can never be realized, they drew the attention of public opinion to the fact that the international relations of States should not be based on arbitrariness and anarchy, but on rules of law and comity. And thereby they have indirectly influenced the gradual growth of rules of law for these international relations.[5]

9.—*The discovery of America an important influence upon the subsequent development of international law.* The new continents provided

---

[1] For the English text, see *Am. Jour. Int. Law,* Vol. 7 (1913), pp. 83–107; and for a comment upon its origin and provisions, see article by Mil. R. Vesnitch in the same *Journal,* pp. 51–82.   [2] Darby, *International Tribunals,* pp. 150–63.
[3] *An Essay on a Congress of Nations,* by William Ladd, reprinted by the Carnegie Endowment for International Peace, Division of International Law (1916).
[4] See Darby, Schücking, and York, previously cited. See also *Schemes for Maintaining General Peace,* by the Rt. Hon. Lord Phillimore, prepared under the direction of the Historical Section of the British Foreign Office, London, 1920.
[5] *International Law* (2d ed.), Vol. I, p. 59, note.

an outlet for the pressure of populations in Europe and offered refuge for the dissatisfied and the oppressed. The riches which flowed from the resources of the new colonies to the Old World replenished the wasted treasuries of its governments and supplied the means for their advancement into great modern states. The law of discovery and occupation had to be interpreted and applied on a larger scale than ever before; conflicting claims of the colonizing nations as to their jurisdiction both on land and on the high seas had to be adjusted; the relations of the Old World colonists to the inhabitants of the New World had to be determined, and not very long thereafter similar questions arose for decision between the colonists in the New World and their home governments in Europe.

This period has in recent years been the subject of special investigation and study by Dr. James Brown Scott, who attributes to the discovery of America "the expansion of international law until it has become a universal rule of conduct." He points out that in the sixteenth century, within forty years after the discovery of America, there was a Spanish school of international law founded by the theologian, Francisco de Vitoria, of the University of Salamanca. The thesis which is upheld by Dr. Scott "proclaims an international community composed of all the nations, the vast majority being the small powers whose defense is righteousness, justice, and the moral standard. It gives to the great expounders of the modern law of nations, who have been silent for centuries, a voice and a control in the development of the science which they founded." [1]

10.—*The American Revolution.* Finally, the American Revolution and the establishment of the first independent government in the New World injected the idea of democratic control into government and in the acts and policies of government; proclaimed the doctrine of government by law and not of men, and laid the foundation for revivifying some of the basic principles of international law as they are now known and accepted. The United States being the first non-European government to be admitted to what had been previously known as the European States System, the terms upon which the new member was admitted had to be determined; after its admittance the new nation advanced its own ideas as to the recognition of governments, non-intervention in the affairs of other governments, and the right to preserve its neutrality in the wars of other nations.

Evidence is not lacking on the plight of European public law at that period. For instance, James Bryce, the English historian of the Holy Roman Empire, writing of the last stage in the decline of the Empire, states that in Germany everything was taken from the sovereign, and

[1] James Brown Scott, *The Spanish Origin of International Law* (1934), Preface.

nothing given to the people, but to the former fief-holders who had become independent potentates; that the Diet, originally an assembly of the people, had become an international congress of diplomatists, and that thereafter the history of the particular states of Germany "is one of the dreariest chapters in the annals of mankind. It would be hard to find," he comments, "from the Peace of Westphalia to the French Revolution, a single grand character or a single noble enterprise; a single sacrifice made to great public interests, a single instance in which the welfare of the people was preferred to the selfish passions of their princes." Nor were these baneful conditions confined to Germany. By the Peace of Westphalia, the fortunes of neighboring countries were linked with those of the Empire. "It was the pivot on which the political system of Europe was to revolve," says Bryce, and, he continues,

the scales, so to speak, which marked the equipoise of power that had become the grand object of the policy of all states. This modern travesty of the plan by which the theorists of the fourteenth century had proposed to keep the world at peace, used means less noble and attained its end no better than theirs had done. No one will deny that it was and is desirable to prevent a universal monarchy in Europe. But it may be asked whether a system can be considered successful which allowed Frederick of Prussia to seize Silesia, which did not check the aggression of Russia and France upon their neighbours, which was for ever bartering and exchanging lands in every part of Europe without thought of the inhabitants, which permitted and was never able to redress such a calamity as the partitionment of Poland.[1]

The revulsion of feeling in the New World was expressed by Henry Wheaton when he characterized the division of Poland as the "most flagrant violation of natural justice and international law which has occurred since Europe emerged from barbarism."[2] Nor was the complaint of the decadence of international law in Europe confined to Anglo-American commentators. The French historian Sorel says that the two episodes which summarized the custom of Europe on the eve of the French Revolution were the War of the Austrian Succession and the division of Poland. He calls these the "testament of Europe" and declares that after this had been signed she could only die, leaving as a legacy the pernicious tradition of the abuses from which she perished.[3]

[1] Bryce, *The Holy Roman Empire* (1921), pp. 395–7.
[2] Wheaton, *History of the Law of Nations* (1845), p. 69.
[3] Albert Sorel, *L'Europe et la révolution française* (1889–1904), Vol. I, p. 89.

CHAPTER II

NATURAL LAW AS A SOURCE OF INTERNATIONAL LAW

So long as the peoples who constituted what we are in the habit of referring to as the "civilized world" were united under the *Pax Romana*, or the Papacy, or the Holy Roman Empire, there was no occasion for, nor could there be, a system of law between them based upon such an institution as the territorial sovereignty of states as that principle is known and understood in modern international law. During these earlier periods of the Christian era, and probably also in the ancient world, there existed customary rights of certain classes of individual strangers not forming a part of the local body politic which, coming down to us from the Roman law, are the sources of the modern international law applicable to the treatment of aliens. But the Reformation served to disrupt both the spiritual and political bonds which held the Western World together under the influence of the centripetal forces of Rome and turned the balance in favor of the centrifugal forces of nationalism whose disintegrating influences were already at work in the Empire. The Peace of Westphalia which ended the thirty years of religous wars abrogated the sovereignty of Rome and transferred political power from the head of the Empire to its members. Following those treaties, between the Alps and the Baltic there were over three hundred petty principalities "each with its own laws, its own court, its little army, its separate coinage, its tolls and custom-houses on the frontier." [1]

Some years ago, the late David Jayne Hill, whose contributions to European diplomatic history have already been referred to, wrote the following paragraph:

The dogs of Constantinople have their own territorial limitations. They follow a stranger to the limit of their wards, but invariably halt upon the frontier with as much deference to the boundary as a French soldier at an outpost of the German Empire. It is not difficult to understand how these limits have been established. Originally, the hungry animals roamed everywhere, seeking after food; but, in time, they fell into habitual rounds, and became attached to certain places where there were exceptional chances for a dinner. Newcomers were attacked and driven away, and these in turn established themselves in less favorable quarters, repelling invasion with a similar ferocity. Thus originated a division of the city into canine wards, or, to change the figure, tribal aggregates were formed, and territorial limits were established by frontier battles, which fixed lines of permanent compromises between the bands of contestants. [2]

[1] Bryce, *The Holy Roman Empire* (1921), pp. 394–5.
[2] Article entitled "International Justice" in the *Yale Law Journal*, October, 1896, p. 1.

The reaction which accompanied the revolutionary change in the political organization of Western Europe by the break-up of the Empire and the emergence of numerous separate sovereignties in its place resulted apparently in reducing that part of the human race almost to the condition of the dogs of Constantinople.   This shocking statement may seem to be an exaggeration unwarranted by the facts, but in support of it, one needs only to peruse authentic accounts of conditions then prevailing.   For instance, the following description of the disastrous effect of the Thirty Years' War on the national life of the times will be perused with horror:

It [the war] had not been carried on by disciplined armies, but by hordes of adventurers whose sole object was plunder. The cruelties they inflicted on their victims are almost beyond conception. Before the war the population was nearly twenty millions; after it the number was probably about six millions. Whole towns and villages were laid in ashes, and vast districts turned into deserts. Churches and schools were closed by hundreds, and to such straits were the people often reduced that cannibalism is said to have been not uncommon. Industry and trade were so completely paralyzed that in 1635 the Hanseatic League was virtually broken up, because the members, once so wealthy, could not meet the necessary expenditure. The population was not only impoverished and reduced in numbers but broken in spirit. It lost confidence in itself, and for a time effected in politics, literature, art and science little that is worthy of serious study.[1]

This desperate state of affairs then obtaining among so-called civilized men was given by Hugo Grotius as one of the principal reasons which induced him to prepare and publish his great work *De Jure Belli ac Pacis*.   In the *Prolegomena* to that work, published in 1625 during the early years of the Thirty Years' War, Grotius thus describes what was passing before his eyes:

Throughout the Christian world I observed a lack of restraint in relation to war, such as even barbarous races should be ashamed of; I observed that men rush to arms for slight causes, or no cause at all, and that when arms have once been taken up there is no longer any respect for law, divine or human; it is as if, in accordance with a general decree, frenzy had openly been let loose for the committing of all crimes. (§ 28)

To restrain the brutal passions which inflame nations in war and to guide and keep them in relations of peace, the great Dutch jurist invoked what he called the Common Law of Nations.

Upon what theory at that stage of the history of nations could Grotius base his assertion that there existed a Common Law of Nations?   He could lay little, if any, stress upon a divine law of nations, for half the world was then arrayed in arms against the other half over the very question of government by divine right.   As for a positive

[1] *Encyclopaedia Britannica* (11th ed.), Vol. XI, p. 860.

law of nations, most of the states were then in the process of throwing off the allegiance which bound them to a higher political authority and of asserting that independent sovereignty upon which the consent of states to positive law is based. Consequently, Grotius was forced to rely, in the main, for the foundation of his Common Law of Nations, upon what he termed natural law, with such discreet allusions to the divine law and the customary law of the Romans as he thought would not prejudice the general reception of his treatise.

What was this natural law upon which Grotius was thus forced to rely in formulating his systematic exposition of a Common Law of Nations? Differences of opinion which arose among the successors of Grotius in expounding the law of nations make such a preliminary inquiry desirable.

The advocates of the law of nature as a source of international law, reasoning by analogy with the supposed primitive state of man, agree that every independent political community is, by virtue of its independence, in a state of nature towards other communities; but they differ in their conception as to what was the state of man in primitive nature. Some assert that he was a contented being at peace with his neighbors and observing the Golden Rule, while others maintain that from the dawn of history man has been engaged in a desperate struggle for existence not only with nature but with his fellow men and is therefore naturally predatory.

The founder of what we may call the "Pure Law of Nature" school was Samuel Pufendorf (1632–1694), who occupied the first chair of the Law of Nature and Nations established in a university, namely, that at Heidelberg. His most important work, *De Jure Naturae et Gentium*, was published in 1672.[1] Pufendorf begins with the proposition that in a state of nature, antecedent to any act of man, all men should be considered as equal, that is, every man should enjoy a natural liberty in which he acts in his own right and is subject to the power of no other man (p. 158); but man, he says, never did live at one and the same time in such a simple state of nature, for, according to Holy Writ, the family relationship began with the creation of man, and "therefore," to quote his words, "a state of nature never actually existed, except in some altered form, or only in part, as when, indeed, some men gathered together with others into a civil state, or some such body, but retained a natural liberty against the rest of mankind; although the more groups there were in this division of the human race, and the smaller their

[1] A photographic reproduction of this work, with an English translation, was published in 1934 by the Carnegie Endowment for International Peace in the series called "The Classics of International Law" (Oxford: Clarendon Press). Pufendorf also published *Elementorum Jurisprudentiae Universalis Libri Duo* in 1660 and *De Officio Hominis et Civis Juxta Legem Naturalem* in 1673. Both works are reproduced in "The Classics of International Law" in the original Latin and English translation.

membership, the nearer it must have approached a pure state of nature." "And so," he adds, "it was not the first men but their descendants who began in fact to live in a state of nature." (p. 163.)

Pufendorf relies upon the origin of the human race, as taught by the Sacred Scriptures, to show that the natural state of men was one of peace rather than war, and that men were more like friends to one another than enemies. Being descended from a single pair of first parents, Pufendorf argues, "the human race is related by no mere general tie of friendship, such as may come from similarity of appearance . . . but by the tie which comes from common ancestry and blood, and which is marked by a kindly affection for one's own." He attributes to forgetfulness man's countless and continuous violations of his blood-bond of affection toward his fellow beings. "A memory of this relationship," he says, "has practically vanished among those who are far removed from the parent stock, and yet, when a man disregards it, and adopts an attitude of hostility towards others, it is proper to feel that he has departed from his primitive and natural state."

Pufendorf explains his assertion that the maintenance of peace toward all men as such is a natural state of man by the statement: "We mean that it has been instituted and sanctioned by nature herself without any human intervention, and that it rests, therefore, upon that obligation of natural law, by which all men are bound, in so far as they are endowed with reason, and which does not owe its original introduction to any convention of men." Following this proposition, Pufendorf shows his disdain for attempts to foist so-called positive law upon the law of nature as, he continues, "it is of no advantage to fortify this universal peace by agreements or treaties; for by a treaty of this nature no addition is made to the obligation of the natural law, that is, the convention does not add anything to which men were not already bound by the very law of nature, nor does it make the obligation more binding." (p. 175.) He confesses, however, "that this natural peace is but a weak and untrustworthy thing, and therefore that it is, without other safeguards, but a poor custodian of man's safety." The powerful forces of man's unbridled passions, he concedes, have led even Christians to the most wicked treacheries, wars, and oppressions; and, therefore, he continues, "the real and principal reason why the fathers of families left their natural liberty and undertook to establish states, was in order that they could surround themselves with defenses against the evils which threaten man from his fellow man." (p. 959.)

But, Pufendorf says in another place, "when at the first mankind separated into different family groups, and now have divided into states, such groups live in a mutual state of nature, in so far as no one group obeys another, and all the members have no common master";

and consequently "commonwealths and their officials may properly claim for themselves the distinction of being in a state of natural liberty." (p. 163.)

Finally, Pufendorf asks the question, whether there be a peculiar and positive law of nations distinct from natural law. We have already mentioned Pufendorf's opinion of treaties which contain only agreements to do what one is already obligated to do or refrain from doing by the natural law. "Every pact, therefore," he says, "must concern something which a man was otherwise unable to require of me by the mere law of nature, or which I was under no perfect obligation beforehand to render to him by the same law." (p. 176.) Custom is likewise rejected by Pufendorf, as unsuited to serve as the source of the universal law of nations because of its inconsistencies and differences among many people (p. 190); but if any custom is based upon the natural law, it has far more dignity than if its origin is based upon the simple agreement of nations (p. 228).

Pufendorf answers in the negative his question whether there be a positive law of nations distinct from the natural law. He agrees with Hobbes,[1] who divides natural law "into the natural law of men and the natural law of states, which is commonly called the law of nations." Pufendorf fully subscribes to Hobbes' statement that "the injunctions of both are the same; but because states, upon being constituted, take on the personal properties of men, the law, which we call natural when speaking of the individual duty of men, on being applied to whole states and nations or peoples, is called the law of nations." This law, Pufendorf holds, is not dependent on the agreement of nations; and moreover he denies "that there is any voluntary or positive law of nations which has the force of law, properly so-called, such as binds nations as if it proceeded from a superior." (p. 226.)

The true basis for the law of nature, he asserts, is found in the condition of man, who cannot exist without leading a social life, and who has been endowed by his Creator with a mind capable of grasping the ideas that lead to this end. The law of nature should, consequently, be deduced from the reason of man himself, and should flow from that source, provided it be not perverted. The fact that most men do not know or understand the method whereby the commands of the law of nature are demonstrated, and that the majority of them usually learn this law and observe it as a matter of training or by following the general example of society, Pufendorf considers no objection to his theory, for this makes it "clear how the fitness of the reason to work out the law of nature may be measured, and on what basis it can be decided whether some command proceeds from a sound or a depraved reason." (p. 203.)

[1] *De Cive*, Chap. XIV, §§ 4, 5.

The obligation of the natural law is of God who, Pufendorf maintains, has bound his creatures to observe it; and its sanction is the reward of good deeds or the punishment of evil ones, either here or hereafter. (p. 217.)

Opposed to the Naturalists is the other school of international law writers, known as the Positivists. They not only defend the existence of a positive law of nations resulting from custom and treaties, but give such positive law precedence over any principles that may be derived from the natural law of nations. The Positivists constituted a large and increasing school of writers. Their leaders in the seventeenth century were two German writers, Rachel and Textor. The former published two dissertations in 1676 entitled *De Jure Naturae et Gentium*, in which he defines the law of nations as the law to which a plurality of free states are subjected, and which comes into existence through the tacit or express consent of these states. Textor published in 1680 a work entitled *Synopsis Juris Gentium*. In the eighteenth century the leadership of the Positive School was assumed by Cornelius van Bynkershoek (1673–1743), a Dutch jurist, who wrote three books dealing separately with different parts of the law of nations. In 1702 he published *De Dominio Maris*, in 1721 *De Foro Legatorum*, and in 1737 *Quaestiones Juris Publici*.[1] According to Bynkershoek, the true basis of the law of nations is the common consent of the nations expressed either in international custom or in treaties.

In the nineteenth century the debate between the Naturalists and the Positivists became heated in England. Richard Wildman, of London, who wrote on the nature and sources of international law in 1849, denied categorically that the law of nature forms any part of international law. He says:

> The term is borrowed from the Roman lawyers. . . . The law of nature in its modern signification means nothing more than natural justice and equity, or the rules of abstract propriety. This was one of its significations in the Roman law. . . . It is obvious that such rules can impose no legal obligations until they are sanctioned by usage or legislative authority, and thus pass into law. Wanting that sanction they bear, when applied to international transactions, the same relation to international law, that the duties of private charity bear to the obligations of municipal law. They are fit to inform the conscience of statesmen, but not to define international rights.[2]

A directly opposite view was expressed in 1883 by James Lorimer, a Scotchman, who defined international law as "the law of nature realized in the relations of separate nations." He explained his point of view by stating his "anxiety to place international law on deeper and more

---

[1] The works of Rachel, Textor, and Bynkershoek are also reproduced in the Carnegie Endowment's "Classics of International Law."

[2] Wildman, *Institutes of International Law*, Vol. I (1849), pp. 2–4.

stable foundations than comity or convention, and to indicate for international jurisprudence the character of a science of nature which I have
elsewhere claimed for jurisprudence as a whole."[1] Lorimer's views
were a few years later supported by Sir Henry Sumner Maine, whose
lectures at Cambridge University in 1887 have been referred to above.[2]

Passing from theory and philosophical thought to the records of
history, we are informed that when the curtain rises which conceals the
dark, prehistoric past, we see fighting everywhere over the earth. The
great kingdoms of antiquity were at war either among themselves or
with the wild hordes descending from the bleak north upon the lands of
sunshine and wealth; the tribes of northern Europe were always at war
with one another, and around the Mediterranean Sea the Greek states
were in constant conflict. The same conditions of natural hostility were
true of the aborigines in Africa and of the Americas when they were
discovered by the white man.[3] Sir Henry Sumner Maine particularly
disagrees with those writers on the origin of international law who think
that mankind started from a condition of innocent peace which was,
they claim, transformed by man's depravity into virtually universal
and unceasing war. "It is not peace," he says, "which was natural
and primitive and old, but rather war. War appears to be as old as
mankind, but peace is a modern invention. Our intelligence is only
just beginning to enable us to penetrate the clouds which rest on the
farther verge of history, but what does seem clear to trained observation
is the universal belligerency of primitive mankind. Not only is war to
be seen everywhere, but it is war more atrocious than we, with our
ideas, can easily conceive."[4]

But let us return to Grotius and see what was his theory of the law of
nature in the law of nations. While he made copious use of the Scriptures and of the poets, he did not undertake to premise the law of nature
upon the blissful state of man in Paradise or in the mythical Golden
Age. As its title indicated, his treatise, universally acknowledged to
be the first systematic general exposition of international law, dealt
primarily with the law of war, and that law is regarded in some quarters
as having been the *raison d'être* of his work. The sections concerning
peace are supposed to have been interpolated into the text of a project
already completely conceived in advance.[5] Grotius, besides being a
philosopher, a theologian, and a poet, was a man of experience in practical affairs, and he did not attempt the impractical task of reviving any
supposed lost Code of the Law of Nature. What he undertook to do

---

[1] Lorimer, *Institutes of the Law of Nations*, Vol. I (1883), pp. vii, 1.
[2] *Supra*, p. 4.   [3] Bryce, *International Relations* (1922), pp. 6–7.
[4] Maine, *International Law* (1888), p. 8.
[5] See introduction by J. B. Scott to the English translation of Grotius published
in "The Classics of International Law" (1925), p. xxvi.

was to set forth a system of law based upon the history and experience of mankind as they were known to him.

Grotius starts from the proposition that the source of the law of nature springs from the need of men for the establishment of a social order and its maintenance upon principles of right reason. Since these characteristic human traits have been implanted in man by his Creator, it follows that the law of nature can also be rightly attributed to divine origin. From the mutual relations of men in society arise bodies of municipal law whose source consequently, in Grotius' opinion, may also be considered as the law of nature. He then argues that "if no association of men can be maintained without law . . . surely also that association which binds together the human race, or binds many nations together, has need of law." He therefore concludes that "just as the laws of each state have in view the advantage of that state, so by mutual consent it has become possible that certain laws should originate as between all states, or a great many states; and it is apparent that the laws thus originating had in view the advantage, not of particular states, but of the greater society of states. And this is what is called the law of nations, whenever we distinguish that term from the law of nature." [1]

There was no dearth of experience in history for Grotius to draw upon in the formulation of his law of war between nations for, from what has been stated previously, it appears that from the earliest times known to man war was a frequent cause of bringing peoples into direct relations with one another. Such relations often called for regulation. "Even in the rudest tribes," we are informed by Bryce, "there was some sort of vague disapproval of certain kinds of behavior, such as the killing of prisoners by torture, massacres upon a great scale, unprovoked attacks upon a harmless tribe, the violation of a promise made in a particularly solemn way." [2]

But Grotius was confronted with a different situation when he came to treat of the law of peace. The only long extended period of peace which civilized man had enjoyed before Grotius was after Rome had conquered the world, had repressed all strife within the limits of her realm and had absorbed the many kingdoms and city states within her gigantic dominion. As pointed out by Bryce, "this unification effected by the conquests of Rome left no international relations subsisting within the empire, though such relations continued to exist with barbarians or semi-civilized people outside. . . ." Although this *Pax Romana* was not a perfect world peace, because there was continuous fighting along some part of the far-flung frontiers of the Empire, or conflicts between rival claimants to the throne, it was, nevertheless,

[1] *Prolegomena*, § 17.   [2] *International Relations* (1922), p. 8.

says Bryce, "a better time than there had ever been before or than there was to come for a long time thereafter." It was this period, beginning shortly before the Christian era, which supplied Grotius with the world's experience upon which to found the international law of peace. That law was known to the Romans themselves as the *ius gentium*, or the *ius naturale*, the two terms being often used synonymously. It had its origin in the undefined status of aliens in Rome who, in the beginning, had no civil rights, either public or private. It grew out of the natural development of the Roman Empire. As nation after nation was added to the Roman dominions, her tribunals were called upon to administer justice to the strangers within her gates who were not subject to the Roman civil law. The Roman courts were thus forced to acquire a knowledge not only of the law of each state added to the Empire, but also of those general principles of justice, fair dealing and good sense which the Romans found to be recognized by other peoples as well as their own, and of giving effect to the usages prevailing among them. These principles the Roman governors subsequently applied in the provinces.

The Roman *ius gentium* was called the law of nations, not in the sense in which the term international law is now used to denote the principles governing the relations between nations, but as being based upon the principles of good faith and equity which underlay and were recognized in the particular law of each community. No part of this Roman law of nations was formally enacted, but the system was built up by the practice of the Roman courts and the action of the Roman jurists. The Romans were not addicted to precision in legal terminology and did not always differentiate between the *ius naturale*, which was based upon reason and convenience and was regarded as superior to other law because it was applicable to all mankind, and the *ius gentium* which, as we have seen, was founded upon the positive law based upon custom and practice prevailing in the various parts of the Empire.

Later, as the nations and nationalities which were added by conquest to the Empire lost their identity as separate civic communities and became blended and ultimately fused in a common subjection to Rome, the exclusive systems of citizenship and law applicable to citizen and provincial became obsolete and they were supplanted by the idea of a community of all mankind embraced within the great Empire which had gathered all civilized men under its wings and had secured for them peace, order, and a just administration of the laws. When such a commonwealth had taken concrete shape in the Roman Empire, there was needed a common law which could be applied to all Roman subjects without regard to citizenship or race and drawing its authority, in accordance with Roman political theory, from the will of the people. The *ius gentium* satisfied these requirements and, being then regarded as coeval with the human race itself, it became considered as having been created by natural reason. From this point the *ius gentium* became practically identical with the *ius naturale*. During the Middle Ages it was engrafted upon the Canon Law and was appealed to by both Pope and Emperor as the only law to which their sovereignties were subject.[1]

The concept of the *ius gentium* upon which Grotius based his systematic treatise on the law of war and peace was stated by his immediate predecessor, the Spanish theologian, Francisco Suárez, whose *Tractatus de Legibus ac Deo Legislatore* appeared in 1612, thirteen years before the great work of Grotius. Suárez classified under the natural law "all the precepts written by God in the hearts of men, and all precepts which may clearly be inferred by reason from natural principles." The precepts of the *ius gentium*, on the other hand, he says, "were introduced by the free will and consent of mankind, whether in the whole human community or in the major portion thereof; consequently, they cannot be said to be written in the hearts of men by the Author of Nature; and therefore they are a part of the human, and not of the natural law."[2]

Grotius cannot be claimed by either the Naturalists or the Positivists as the founder of their particular school of international law. The distinction which he makes between the natural and the positive or voluntary law of nations is not the same as that drawn, for instance, by Pufendorf in behalf of the Naturalists; nor does Grotius base his systematic treatise on the law of nations exclusively upon the consent of nations as do the Positivists.

The influence of Grotius dominated the writers of the seventeenth and eighteenth centuries. His disciples occupied a position midway between the Naturalists and Positivists. They maintain the distinction between the natural and the voluntary law of nations and consider both of equal importance.

The most outstanding of the Grotians was Christian Wolff (1679–1754), a German philosopher who was first professor of mathematics and philosophy in the Universities of Halle and Marburg and afterwards returned to the former university as professor of the law of nations. In 1749, when seventy years of age, he published his *Jus Gentium Methodo Scientifica Pertractatum*.[3] Reasoning from the existence of a family of

---

[1] For authorities on the preceding summary of the development of the *ius gentium* and natural law, see Henry Wheaton, *History of the Law of Nations* (1845), Introduction; James Bryce, *Studies in History and Jurisprudence* (1901), Chap. XI, also *International Relations* (1922), Lect. 1; Sir Frederick Pollock, *Essays in the Law* (1922), Sec. II.

[2] *The Spanish Conception of International Law and of Sanctions*, by James Brown Scott, p. 77. (Pamphlet No. 54, Carnegie Endowment for International Peace, 1934.)

[3] This work (text of 1764) was republished in 1934 in "The Classics of International Law" by the Carnegie Endowment for International Peace in a photographic reproduction of the original Latin and in English translation.

nations, Wolff contended that the totality of states forms a world state, the so-called *civitas gentium maxima*, above the component member states. He distinguishes four different kinds of law of nations: the natural, the voluntary, the customary, and that which is expressly created by treaties. Customary and treaty law have force only between the states whose custom and treaties have created them and may be altered by those states; but the natural and the voluntary law of nations are eternal, unchangeable and universally binding upon all the states. In contradistinction to Grotius, who calls the customary law of nations "voluntary," Wolff denominates "voluntary" those rules of the law of nations which are tacitly imposed by the *civitas gentium maxima* upon member states.

Emerich de Vattel (1714–1767), a Swiss from Neuchâtel, who entered the service of Saxony and became her minister at Berne, undertook to introduce Wolff's teachings into the diplomacy of Europe. In 1758 he published *Le droit des gens ou Principes de la loi naturelle appliqués à la conduite et aux affaires des nations et des souverains.*[1] The work of Vattel considerably influenced the early conceptions of international law in the United States. For example, James Kent, an early commentator on American law, wrote that "when the United States ceased to be a part of the British Empire, and assumed the character of an independent nation, they became subject to that system of rules which reason, morality, and custom had established among the civilized nations of Europe, as their public law. . . . By this law," Kent continues, "we are to understand that code of public instruction which defines the rights and prescribes the duties of nations, in their intercourse with each other." Kent notes the difference of opinion among writers concerning the foundation of the law of nations. "It has been considered by some," he says, "as a mere system of positive institutions, founded upon consent and usage; while others have insisted that it was essentially the same as the law of nature, applied to the conduct of nations, in the character of moral persons, susceptible of obligations and laws." Commenting upon this difference of opinion, Kent states that "we are not to adopt either of these theories as exclusively true. The most useful and practical part of the law of nations is, no doubt, instituted or positive law, founded on usage, consent, and agreement. But it would be improper to separate this law entirely from natural jurisprudence, and not to consider it as deriving much of its force and dignity from the same principles of right reason, the same views of the nature and constitution of man, and the same sanction of

[1] This work was republished in 1916 in "The Classics of International Law" by the Carnegie Institution of Washington. Two volumes contain a photographic reproduction of the French text, while an English translation is included in the third volume.

divine revelation, as those from which the science of morality is de-duced." Kent concludes that "there is a natural and a positive law of nations. By the former, every state, in its relations with other states, is bound to conduct itself with justice, good faith, and benevolence; and this application of the law of nature has been called by Vattel the neces-sary law of nations, because nations are bound by the law of nature to observe it; and it is termed by others the internal law of nations, be-cause it is obligatory upon them in point of conscience." [1]

Regardless of the view one may take of the present relation of natural to positive law, the history of the evolution of the science of inter-national law contains support for the following propositions:

First, at its birth and during the infancy of international law, the law of nature was an important source and an indispensable guide. In its earliest years, when the law of nations was so largely confined to the law of war, natural law exerted its greatest influence in ameliorating the inhuman practices of primitive war. In referring to this period, Sir Henry Sumner Maine, in his Cambridge lectures, already mentioned, says that "the greatest function of the law of nature was discharged in giving birth to modern international law and the modern law of war." [2] And Oppenheim, also previously quoted, pays this tribute to the in-fluence of the law of nature upon the development of international law:

Whatever we may nowadays think of this Law of Nature, the fact remains unshaken that for more than two hundred years after Grotius, jurists, philoso-phers, and theologians firmly believed in it. And there is no doubt that, but for the system of the Law of Nature and the doctrines of its prophets, the modern Constitutional Law and the modern Law of Nations would not be what they actually are. The Law of Nature supplied the crutches with whose help history has taught mankind to walk out of the institutions of the Middle Ages into those of modern times. [3]

Secondly, in the adolescence of international law as an accepted system governing the relations of modern sovereign states, conflicts occur between concepts based upon the law of nature and principles flowing from the theory of the consent of nations. In such conflicts natural law theories usually are subordinated to the more pressing de-mands of material considerations. A leading case involving such a conflict came before the Supreme Court of the United States over a century ago and was decided by the great American Chief Justice, John Marshall. [4] This case arose out of the capture by an American cruiser of an American vessel which was charged with piratically seizing slaves

[1] Kent, *Commentaries on American Law* (1826), Vol. I, p. 2.
[2] Maine, *International Law* (1888), p. 8.
[3] Oppenheim, *International Law* (2d ed.), Vol. I, p. 87.
[4] *The Antelope* (1825), 10 Wheaton, 66; Dickinson, *A Selection of Cases and Other Readings on the Law of Nations* (1929), p. 20; Fenwick, *Cases on International Law* (1935), p. 7.

from Spanish and Portuguese ships engaged in the slave trade. The vessel was brought into a United States port for condemnation under American law, where the United States Government sought to free the Africans on the ground that slave-trading was against the law of nature and therefore condemned by the law of nations. The Spanish and Portuguese Consuls claimed the slaves as the property of subjects of their nations. Chief Justice Marshall could not deny that slavery is contrary to the law of nature, for, he said: "That every man has a natural right to the fruits of his own labour, is generally admitted; and that no other person can rightfully deprive him of those fruits, and appropriate them against his will, seems to be the necessary result of this admission. But," he continued,

from the earliest times war has existed, and war confers rights in which all have acquiesced. Among the most enlightened nations of antiquity, one of these was, that the victor might enslave the vanquished. This, which was the usage of all, could not be pronounced repugnant to the law of nations, which is certainly to be tried by the test of general usage. That which has received the assent of all, must be the law of all.

Slavery, then, has its origin in force; but as the world has agreed that it is a legitimate result of force, the state of things which is thus produced by general assent, cannot be pronounced unlawful.

Throughout Christendom, this harsh rule has been exploded, and war is no longer considered as giving a right to enslave captives. But this triumph of humanity has not been universal. The parties to the modern law of nations do not propagate their principles by force; and Africa has not yet adopted them. Throughout the whole extent of that immense continent, so far as we know its history, it is still the law of nations that prisoners are slaves. Can those who have themselves renounced this law, be permitted to participate in its effect by purchasing the beings who are its victims?

Whatever might be the answer of a moralist to this question, a jurist must search for its legal solution, in those principles of action which are sanctioned by the usages, the natural acts, and the general assent, of that portion of the world of which he considers himself as a part, and to whose law the appeal is made. If we resort to this standard as the test of international law, the question, as has already been observed, is decided in favour of the legality of the trade. Both Europe and America embarked in it; and for nearly two centuries, it was carried on without opposition, and without censure. A jurist could not say, that a practice thus supported was illegal, and that those engaged in it might be punished, either personally, or by deprivation of property.

Marshall concluded his decision with the famous quotation proclaiming the equality of states and the legal corollary that no nation can make law except for itself. He said:

In this commerce, thus sanctioned by universal assent, every nation had an equal right to engage. How is this right to be lost? Each may renounce it for its own people; but can this renunciation affect others?

No principle of general law is more universally acknowledged, than the perfect equality of nations. Russia and Geneva have equal rights. It results from this equality, that no one can rightfully impose a rule on another. Each legislates for itself, but its legislation can operate on itself alone. A right, then, which is vested in all by the consent of all, can be divested only by consent; and this trade, in which all have participated, must remain lawful to those who cannot be induced to relinquish it. As no nation can prescribe a rule for others, none can make a law of nations; and this traffic remains lawful to those whose governments have not forbidden it.

Another and different kind of example might be cited. In his essay entitled *Perpetual Peace*, published in 1795, Immanuel Kant objected to the phrase "international law" as being "without substance, since it depends upon treaties which contain in the very act of their conclusion the reservation of their breach." [1] This is a bald and uncompromising statement of the attitude of those who would deny any influence to natural law in the law governing the conduct of nations toward one another. But let us oppose to this statement the view of the Spanish theologian Suárez, who wrote nearly two centuries before Kant. The obligation to observe treaties, he said, pertains to the natural law and does not rest upon the *ius gentium;* but since, nevertheless, compliance with treaties receives additional support from custom and the law of nations, the subject may be included under the head of *ius gentium* in the strict sense of the term. [2]

These two opposing viewpoints of the seventeenth and eighteenth centuries were subjected to the acid test of the World War in 1914. Notwithstanding that the neutrality of Luxemburg and Belgium had been guaranteed by treaties to which Germany was a party, her troops occupied both countries. Kant's philosophy thus seemed to be vindicated, as likewise seemed justified the approval of Bismarck, who, in his *Reflections*, says that "no treaty can guarantee the degree of zeal and the amount of force that will be devoted to the discharge of obligations when the private interest of those who lie under them no longer reinforces the text and its earliest interpretation." [3] But while the law as stated by Suárez was impotent to withstand the guns which besieged Liége, yet above their roar the world heard, and long after the war remembers the words of the German Chancellor von Bethmann-Hollweg, who proclaimed in the Reichstag in Berlin on August 4, 1914, "This is against the law of nations. . . . The injustice which we thus commit we will repair as soon as our military object has been attained." [4]

As to this struggle between the ideals of natural justice, on the one hand, and, on the other, the requirements of positive law founded upon the consent of states for safeguarding their own interests, we can do no

---

[1] *Zum ewigen Frieden*, quoted by Phillips in *The Confederation of Europe* (1914), p. 5.
[2] Suárez, *Tractatus de Legibus ac Deo Legislatore* (1612).
[3] *Reflections and Reminiscences*, English translation (1898), Vol. II, p. 270, cited by Phillips, *op. cit.*, p. 5.
[4] *Am. Jour. Int. Law*, Vol. 9 (1915), p. 77.

better than to close with the following statement of the English author, Sir Robert Phillimore, written more than eighty years ago:

In the great community of the world, in the society of societies, states are placed in relations with each other, as individuals are with each other in the particular society to which they belong. . . . As it is ordained by God that the individual man should attain to the full development of his faculties through his intercourse with other men, and that so a people should be formed, so it is divinely appointed that each individual society should reach that degree of perfection of which it is capable, through its intercourse with other societies. To move, and live, and have its being in the great community of nations, is as much the normal condition of a single nation, as to live in a social state is the normal condition of a single man.

From the nature then of states, as from the nature of individuals, certain rights and obligations towards each other necessarily spring; these are defined and governed by certain laws. These are the laws which form the bond of justice between nations, and which are the subject of international jurisprudence, and the science of the international lawyer.

To clothe with reality the abstract idea of justice, to secure by law within its own territories the maintenance of right against aggression of the individual wrong-doer, is the primary object of the state, the great duty of each separate society. To secure by law, throughout the world, the maintenance of right against the aggression of the national wrong-doer, is the primary object of the commonwealth of states, and the great duty of the society of societies. Obedience to the law is as necessary for the liberty of states as it is for the liberty of individuals.[1]

[1] Phillimore, *International Law* (3d ed.), Vol. I, pp. 3-5.

CHAPTER III

MODERN TEXT-WRITERS ON INTERNATIONAL LAW

In the preceding chapter we have cited and otherwise referred to the more important publicists in international law from Hugo Grotius to Vattel, corresponding to the early period of modern international law which began with the Peace of Westphalia and lasted up to about the time of the independence of the United States of America and its admission to what, till then, had been a European Family of Nations. This event started what may be regarded as a renaissance in modern international law, evidenced by the appearance of numerous writers from many different countries, who have enlarged its literature in ever increasing diversity and proportions to the present time; before mentioning particular authors, it would seem advisable to make some general comment upon the value of text-writers as authorities.

Oppenheim has called attention to the reason why text-books of international law have so much more importance for the application of the law than text-books of other branches of the law, namely, the absence in the sphere of international law of an organized judiciary such as exists in municipal law for ascertaining and interpreting the law involved in a controverted case. He says, "The writers on international law, and in especial the authors of treatises, have in a sense to take the places of the judges and have to pronounce whether there is an established custom or not, whether there is a usage only in contradistinction to a custom, whether a recognized usage has now ripened into a custom, and the like." And with regard to the written rules of international law which may be the outcome of universal or general law-making treaties, Oppenheim says, "The writers have again to take the place of the judges and have to ascertain the precise meaning of those rules with the help of interpretation." [1]

Wheaton, writing in 1836, places text-writers of authority in the first place as sources of international law. They show, he says, "what is the approved usage of nations, or the general opinion respecting their mutual conduct, with the definitions and modifications introduced by general consent. Without wishing to exaggerate the importance of these writings," Wheaton continues, "or to substitute, in any case, their authority for the principles of reason, it may be affirmed that they are generally impartial in their judgment. They are witnesses of the sentiments and usages of civilized nations, and the weight of their testi-

[1] L. Oppenheim, "The Science of International Law," *Am. Jour. Int. Law*, Vol. 2 (1908), p. 315.

mony increases every time that their authority is invoked by statesmen, and every year that passes without the rules laid down in their works being impugned by the avowal of contrary principles."[1]

Thomas A. Walker, commenting upon Wheaton's statement, states that the information of the text-writer is commonly second-hand, and observes:

Text writers, when they do their duty, are simply the impartial historians of International Law. To them it belongs to note actual facts and events, and to extract from them broad principles for the future guidance of mankind. The authority they possess, they possess not as judges, but as skilled observers and relaters, and that authority will increase or decrease, accordingly, according as their representations present, or do not present, an accurate picture of actual practice. When the text writer becomes a theorist, it is time for men to look askance at his opinion; and when he becomes, as he too often does become, the advocate of the special view of a particular people, his arguments must be treated as the arguments of counsel in a court of law. Greater authority is wont to be assigned on the Continent to the opinions of jurists than in England and America, but even in English and American courts the views of certain writers, more particularly the authorities of the classic period from Grotius to Vattel, are at times freely cited in support of special arguments. In the end, nevertheless, the text writer is a good witness, and speaks with convincing authority, when he speaks of past facts, not when he ventures upon moral advice. Gentilis, Grotius, Puffendorf, Zouch, Bynkershoek, Leibnitz, Wolf, Vattel and the rest, were great men in their generation, but they were not advisedly makers of law. Their opinions may have passed, and undoubtedly in many cases did insensibly pass, into the opinion of their age, and became reflected in practice, but that honour they owed to the strength of their intellect and the soundness of their appreciation of the moral needs of their time. And their successors are in like case.[2]

Sir William Vernon Harcourt, in his "Letters by Historicus on Some Questions of International Law," printed in the London *Times* in 1863 during the American Civil War, after examining the writers on international law, made the following comment on them:

The text-writer on international law assumes a noble task, but he at the same time accepts a grave responsibility. His speculations, if unsound, and his maxims, if unjustifiable, must too often be refuted by the sword. They furnish pretexts sometimes for unjust demands, at others for unrighteous refusals. Those who assume the authority of Publicists exercise, in some sort, the judicial functions of life and death. Like the Feciales of old, of whose office they are the legitimate heirs, they deal out the lots of peace and of war; and thereby, according as they guide or pervert the judgments of their age, they affect the destinies of nations and determine the misery or the happiness of whole generations of mankind.[3]

Chancellor Kent earlier in his *Commentaries*,[4] had said that "in cases where the principal jurists agree, the presumption will be very

[1] *Elements of International Law* (Dana ed., 1866), pp. 23–4.
[2] *A History of the Law of Nations* (1899), Vol. I, pp. 21–2.
[3] *Letters by Historicus*, pp. v–vi.   [4]Vol. I, p. 19.

great in favor of the solidity of their maxims; and no civilized nation
that does not arrogantly set all ordinary law and justice at defiance will
venture to disregard the uniform sense of the established writers of
international law."

Quoting with approval the foregoing statement, Phillimore continues:

If the authority of Zouch, of Lee, of Mansfield, and, above all, of Stowell, be
against the demand of England—if Valin, Domat, Pothier, and Vattel be opposed to the pretensions of France—if Grotius and Bynkershoek confute the
claim of Holland—Puffendorf that of Sweden—if Heineccius, Leibnitz, and
Wolff array themselves against Germany—if Story, Wheaton, and Kent condemn
the act of America, it cannot be supposed (except, indeed, in the particular
epoch of a Revolution, when all regard to law is trampled under foot) that the
argumentum ad patriam would not prevail—at all events, it cannot be doubted
that it *ought* to prevail, and should the country relying upon such authority be
compelled to resort to arms, that the guilt of the War would rest upon the an-
tagonist refusing to be bound by it.[1]

Supposing, however, there is not agreement among the writers, but
differences of opinion between them concerning a given custom or
principle, what value is to be ascribed to the various opinions?   Phillimore says it is impossible to lay down a precise rule, "but among the
criteria of it will be the length of time by which it is, as it were, con-
secrated, the period when it was expressed, the reasoning upon which it
rests, the usage by which it has been since strengthened and to the
previous existence of which it testifies." [2]

The Supreme Court of the United States in 1900 judicially decided
the place of the text-writer as an authority in international law.   Said
that court, speaking through Mr. Justice Gray:

Where there is no treaty, and no controlling executive or legislative act or
judicial decision, resort must be had to the customs and usages of civilized nations; and, as evidence of these, to the works of jurists and commentators, who
by years of labor, research and experience, have made themselves peculiarly well
acquainted with the subjects of which they treat.   Such works are resorted to by
judicial tribunals, not for the speculations of their authors concerning what the
law ought to be, but for trustworthy evidence of what the law really is.[3]

It would be quite beyond our scope and purpose to discuss or even to
mention all of the writers on international law during the period from
Vattel to the present.   This period has been marked by the appearance
of a multiplicity of volumes dealing with special topics of international
law, as well as a surprisingly large number of general treatises on the
subject.   It will be practicable to state briefly the careers, in such a

---

[1] *International Law* (3d ed.), Vol. I, pp. 64–65.   [2] *Ibid.*, p. 63.
[3] *Paquete Habana*, 175 U. S. 677; Dickinson, *Cases and Other Readings on the Law of
Nations* (1929), p. 42; Fenwick, *Cases on International Law* (1935), p. 12; Scott,
Cases on International Law (1922), pp. 12 and 17.

way as to indicate the authority which they may possess, of the authors of only the more important works in the latter class.[1]

GEORGES FRÉDÉRIC DE MARTENS (1756–1821). De Martens, professor of law in the University of Göttingen, published a number of books on the law of nations. His most important one entitled *Précis du droit des gens moderne de l'Europe, fondé sur les traités et l'usage* was published in 1789 and was therefore contemporaneous with the entry of the United States into the family of nations. Born at Hamburg in 1756, he was made counsellor to the King of Westphalia in 1808; seven years later he was counsellor in the cabinet of the King of Hanover, and subsequently he represented that sovereign in the Diet of the Germanic Confederation. He died in 1821. Chancellor Kent, a contemporary writer, states that Martens' *Précis* of the law of nations is a treatise of great practical utility but gives only a very partial view of the system because it was confined to the customary and conventional law of the modern nations of Europe. [2] Wheaton, who wrote a half century later, says that the work of De Martens "has become a justly esteemed manual of the science." [3] Ten years later, Sir Robert Phillimore stated that De Martens' work "has obtained, not undeservedly, a place among the classics of international law." [4] In 1905, Oppenheim wrote that "the influence of Martens was great, and even at the present time is considerable." [5]

The work was translated into English by Mr. William Cobbett and published at Philadelphia in 1795. The publisher, James Bradford, inserted a dedication to George Washington, President of the United States of America, in which he paid tribute to the part played by President Washington in guiding the young republic during the momentous period of its infancy in the family of nations.

JAMES KENT (1763–1847). In the same month and year in which John Jay signed in London the treaty which bears his name, i.e., November, 1794, James Kent began to lecture on law in Columbia College (now Columbia University) in the City of New York. In 1795, a volume of eighty-seven pages was issued by the trustees of the college containing three preliminary dissertations by Professor Kent discussing the constitutional history of the United States and important principles of the law of nations. In 1796, Kent was appointed by Governor Jay of New York, the same who negotiated the Jay Treaty, one of the two masters in chancery of the state. With his career as chancellor we shall go no farther. Having retired from public office in the summer of

---

[1] An excellent and complete list of authorities, classical and modern, with brief comments upon each, may be found in Ernest Nys, *Le droit international* (1912), Vol. I, Chap. IX, pp. 224–351.   [2] Kent, *Commentaries*, Vol. I, p. 18.
[3] Wheaton, *History of the Law of Nations* (1845), p. 325.
[4] Phillimore, *International Law* (3d ed.), Vol. I, p. xxv.
[5] Oppenheim, *International Law* (2d ed.), Vol. I, p. 92.

1823, Chancellor Kent received another appointment as professor of law from the trustees of Columbia College. A summary of his first ten lectures was published in 1824, and in 1826 there appeared the first of the four volumes entitled *Commentaries on American Law*, containing the lectures delivered by Kent under his professorship. These volumes were destined to serve as a standard general treatise on law in the United States, occupying in this country a position similar to that of Blackstone's *Commentaries on the Common Law in England*. The foundation and history of the law of nations were of great interest to Professor Kent for they were the subject of one of his first lectures. The value of the contributions to international law by Chancellor Kent, who was a legal adviser of the statesmen who shaped the international policy of the young republic, was later stated by competent citizens of the mother country.

Sir William Vernon Harcourt, in his letters to the London *Times*, after making the statement in regard to the value of text-writers, above quoted, proceeded to emphasize his opinion of the worth of Chancellor Kent's work in the following language:

Permit me, while I am warning your readers against false lights, to refer them to a guide who will never lead them astray—to the greatest jurist whom this age has produced—I mean the American Chancellor Kent. Of his writings it may be safely said that they are never wrong. The exposition of international law contained in the first volume of the *Commentaries* has but one fault—that of being too short.[1]

Shortly thereafter, in 1866, a volume entitled *Kent's Commentary on International Law* appeared in London with the following explanation by its editor, J. T. Abdy, judge of county courts, former Regius professor of law in the University of Cambridge, and then law professor at Gresham College:

Chancellor Kent has given us the result of years of professional labour, and a life spent in study, in a work which, if small so far as International Law is concerned, contains within its pages wisdom, critical skill, and judicial acumen of the highest kind. . . .
I have therefore selected that portion of his Commentaries which relates to public International Law, and have edited it as a separate volume, . . . because no other writer on International Law is so safe, so impartial, and so recognized a guide and authority, whether in this country, or on the continent of Europe, or across the Atlantic.[2]

JEAN LOUIS KLÜBER (1762–1836). In 1819 Klüber published in French at Stuttgart *Droit des gens moderne de l'Europe*. Two years later a revised and enlarged edition was published in German under the title *Europäisches Völkerrecht*.

[1] *Letters by Historicus*, p. 129.
[2] Preface to Abdy, *Kent's International Law*, 1st ed., p. iv.

Klüber was born in Alsace in 1762, and became professor of law at the University of Erlangen where he became known as a commentator on the constitution of the Holy Roman Empire. In 1807 he was called to Heidelberg, and in the following year accepted the position of counsellor to the Grand Duke of Baden. With the permission of his government, he went to Vienna and remained there during the Congress of 1815. Through his relations with the diplomats there, he obtained a great number of documents, some of them secret, showing the history and work of that epoch-making assemblage. These he used in compiling his nine-volume collection of the Acts of the Congress of Vienna and his review of the negotiations of the congress. His experience and practical knowledge thus acquired were utilized in the preparation of his later treatise on international law. Several editions of it have appeared since Klüber's death in 1836, the last being that edited by M. A. Ott and published in Paris in 1874.

ANDRÉS BELLO (1780–1865). The next author whom we shall notice in point of time was neither a European nor a North American, but a South American, born in Venezuela, who became distinguished in the service of Chile. Bello was attached to the legation sent to London by the Supreme Junta established at Caracas in 1810 to maintain the communications of the South American revolutionists with Great Britain. The head of this legation was none other than the then Colonel Simon Bolívar, later General, who became the great South American Liberator. In 1822 Bello was made secretary of the Chilean Legation in London, and in 1824, he was given the same official position for Colombia. After nineteen years in the diplomatic service in London, Bello in 1829 was called to service in Chile, where he was first adviser and secretary in the Ministry of Foreign Relations and later head of that department from 1834 to 1855. His work in Spanish entitled *Principios de derecho de gentes* appeared in 1832. In the foreword of this work Bello acknowledged his indebtedness to James Kent's *Commentaries*. Bello founded and was the first president of the University of Chile, he was the author of the civil code of that country, and is credited with establishing the jurisprudence of the Chilean Foreign Office. The third edition of this work, enlarged and revised by the author, was published posthumously in 1873. In 1872 the National Congress of Chile passed a law authorizing the publication under the direction of the Council of Public Instruction of the complete works of Bello. Volume X of this series, entitled *Derecho internacional*, was published in Santiago de Chile in 1886. Calvo referred to Bello as the precursor of Henry Wheaton, who will be our next author to be noted.

HENRY WHEATON (1785–1848). In 1836, what is now regarded as an American classic of international law appeared from the pen of

Henry Wheaton entitled *Elements of International Law*, with a sketch of the history of the science. Wheaton was born in Providence, Rhode Island, in 1785, studied law, and became a member of the bar. He also studied abroad, where he became familiar with foreign languages, history, and literature. From 1815 to 1819, he was a justice of the Marine Court of New York. He published a *Digest of the Law of Maritime Captures* in 1815. From 1816 to 1827, Wheaton was the official reporter of the United States Supreme Court and edited twelve volumes of reports of that court. He left the Supreme Court to accept the position of chargé d'affaires of the United States to Denmark, where he took part in the settlement of the Sound Dues question. From 1837 to 1846 he was Minister to Prussia and, upon his return to the United States in the latter year, he became lecturer on international law at Harvard University. He died in 1848.

Wheaton's *Elements of International Law* has passed through many editions and translations. In 1864, it was translated into Chinese by order of the Chinese Government under the direction of the Reverend W. A. P. Martin, an American missionary, and used as a text-book for its officials. It was also adapted from the Chinese for use in Japan, where it was published in six volumes in Tokyo in 1865. The eighth American edition, edited with valuable notes by Richard Henry Dana, was published in 1866. The sixth English edition, revised, enlarged and rewritten by A. Berriedale Keith, was published in London in 1929. The volume has also passed through Spanish, Italian, and French editions. A centenary memorial edition, consisting of a literal reproduction of the eighth American edition by Dana, was published in 1936 by the Carnegie Endowment for International Peace, with an introduction and notes by Professor George Grafton Wilson, of Harvard University.

Wheaton is also the author of a noteworthy *History of the Law of Nations*, published in French in 1841 and in English in 1845.

AUGUST WILHELM HEFFTER (1796–1880). In 1844 *Das europäische Völkerrecht* was published in Berlin and it has since taken its place among the important modern contributions. Oppenheim says that "in exact application of the juristic method, Heffter's book excels all former ones, and all the following authors are in a sense standing on his shoulders." [1] Heffter was born in 1796 in that part of Saxony which was later incorporated into Prussia. He was a professor successively at the Universities of Bonn, Halle, and Berlin. His work has been translated into several languages. The French edition of 1883 and the eighth German edition of 1888 are enriched with valuable notes by F. Heinrich Geffcken, who states that the merit of the work is that it presents

[1] *International Law* (2d ed.), Vol. I, p. 98.

with legal precision a picture of international law as it exists, divorced from all political metaphysics.

SIR ROBERT PHILLIMORE (1810–1885). The four volumes entitled *Commentaries upon International Law* appeared from 1854 to 1861, and no well-equipped library of international law would now be complete without them. Again we quote Oppenheim's opinion, who says that "generations to come will consult Phillimore's volumes on account of the vast amount of material they contain and the sound judgment they exhibit." Phillimore was an English lawyer who was appointed queen's advocate in 1862 and admiralty judge in 1867. The third edition of his volumes appeared from 1879 to 1888.

THEODORE DWIGHT WOOLSEY (1801–1889). Dr. Woolsey's *Introduction to the Study of International Law* appeared in 1860. It was designed by the author as an aid in teaching and in historical studies. Woolsey was born in 1801 and became a Congregational minister. In 1846 he was elected president of Yale College, which position he retained until 1871. The sixth edition, revised and enlarged by his son, Theodore S. Woolsey, appeared in 1891. Woolsey's original volume was translated into Chinese.

HENRY W. HALLECK (1815–1872). Two volumes entitled *International Law* were published in 1861. Sir Sherston Baker became the editor of future editions, the fourth of which, revised and rewritten, was published in 1908. Halleck's work is especially valuable in its treatment of the laws of war because of the experience of the author, who had a distinguished career in the United States Army. A graduate of West Point, he saw service in the Mexican and Civil Wars. He was secretary of state under the military government in California, but resigned from the Army in 1854 to practice law in that state. Upon the outbreak of the Civil War, he returned to the Army as a major general. He served in command of the western theatre of war and later as general in chief at Washington. Upon being replaced by General Grant, Halleck was made chief of staff, and his influence on the conduct of the Civil War is said to have been greater than that of any soldier on either side save Grant and Lee. It was while General Halleck was commander in chief that Dr. Francis Lieber was assigned the task of preparing his famous *Instructions for the Government of the Armies in the Field*. These instructions were submitted to and approved by General Halleck before they were adopted by President Lincoln and issued as General Orders No. 100 in 1863. In a letter to General Halleck, Dr. Lieber expressed regret that Halleck's name was not visibly connected with the instructions.[1]

PASQUALE FIORE (1837–1914). The first systematic treatise on in-

[1] *Am. Jour. Int. Law*, Vol. I (1907), p. 20.

ternational law published in Italy appeared in 1865, under the title
Nuovo diritto internazionale pubblico, and was from the pen of Fiore,
who was born in Italy in 1837 and was professor of international law at
the Universities of Urbino (1863–65), Pisa (1867–75), Turin (1875–80),
and Naples (from 1881 to his death in 1914). In later life Fiore was
a senator of Italy. The fourth edition of his work appeared in two
volumes in 1904–5. It has been translated into French and Spanish.
Fiore is also the author of a work entitled *Il diritto internazionale codificato*, the first edition of which appeared in 1890 and the fifth in 1915.
This work has been translated into French and English. The latter
translation, by Professor Edwin Borchard, of Yale University, was
published in 1918.

JOHANN CASPAR BLUNTSCHLI (1808–1881), a Swiss jurist and politi-
cian. Born at Zurich in 1808, he became professor at the university of
that city upon its foundation in 1833. His participation in the political
strife between the Swiss cantons caused him to remove to Germany,
where he became professor of constitutional law at the University of
Munich in 1848. In 1861, he was called to the same chair at Heidelberg, where he became interested in international law in trying to keep
Baden neutral during the Austro-Prussian War of 1866. In that year
he published *Das moderne Kriegsrecht*, and in 1868 *Das moderne Völkerrecht*. The third edition appeared in 1878, and the fifth edition of a
French translation in 1895. He was one of the founders of the *Institut
de Droit International* and represented Germany at the Brussels
Conference of 1874 on the Revision of the Laws of War.

Bluntschli and Lieber were old friends, the latter having been forced
to emigrate from Germany to the United States for political reasons.
In Bluntschli's miscellaneous writings he pays tribute to Lieber's *Instructions* as "a deed of great moment in the history of international law and
of civilization" and states that "these instructions, prepared by Lieber,
prompted me to draw up, after his model, first, the laws of war, and
then, in general, the law of nations, in the form of a code, or law book,
which should express the present state of the legal consciousness of
civilized peoples. Lieber, in his correspondence with me, had strongly
urged that I should do this, and lent me continual encouragement." [1]

CARLOS CALVO (1824–1906). Calvo is an outstanding Latin American publicist who has written upon modern international law. His
original work, which was in Spanish, appeared in 1868 under the title
Derecho internacional teórico y práctico de Europa y América. Calvo
was born at Buenos Aires in 1824 and entered the consular service of the
Argentine Republic in 1852. In 1860 he was sent by Paraguay on
special mission to London and Paris. He was later Argentine Minister

[1] *Am. Jour. Int. Law*, Vol. 1 (1907), p. 23.

at St. Petersburg, Vienna, Berlin, and Paris, and was one of the founders of the *Institut de Droit International*. Subsequent editions of his work have been in French, the fifth edition in six volumes having been published in 1896.

Calvo is the author of the doctrine bearing his name which condemns diplomatic as well as armed intervention for the collection of private claims of a purely pecuniary nature based upon contract or growing out of civil war, insurrection, or mob violence. This principle has been largely adopted as part of the public law of the Latin American states, being incorporated in the constitution and laws of many of those countries. Provisions known as the Calvo Clause have been inserted in many contracts and concessions granted to foreigners in Latin America, under which the grantee or concessionaire agrees to assume the position of a national of the contracting government in matters growing out of the contract or concession and renounces the diplomatic intervention of his own government.[1] The Calvo Doctrine is to be distinguished from the Drago Doctrine, a principle which forbids the forcible collection of public debts, proposed by the Minister for Foreign Affairs of Argentina during the intervention of the European powers in Venezuela in 1902 and later given general international approval at the Hague Conference in 1907. There have been many interpretations of the effect of the Calvo Clause by international mixed commissions.

THÉOPHILE FUNCK-BRENTANO and ALBERT SOREL. A volume appeared over the joint names of these two in 1877 entitled *Précis du droit des gens*. Funck-Brentano was born in Luxembourg in 1830, and Sorel in France in 1842. The former was professor at the *Ecole Libre des Sciences Politiques* in Paris, and the latter a member of the French Academy. Their work was crowned by the Academy. The authors divided international law into what they called theoretical and actual. The former, they said, consists of the speculations of writers preoccupied with the good of humanity and the progress of civilization, and stands in regard to the actual relations of nations in the same position as natural law stands in the actual relations of individuals. They asserted that actual international law grew out of the relations which exist between nations because of their intercourse with each other and is founded on custom and conventions. Nys describes the work as more of a treatise on European politics than a book of law. Both authors died in 1906.

WILLIAM EDWARD HALL (1835–1894). Hall's treatise on *International Law*, published in 1880, is one of the later outstanding books in the English language. The eighth edition, edited by Dr. A. Pearce Higgins, of Cambridge University, was published in 1924. Hall was

[1] See H. Arias, *Am. Jour. Int. Law*, Vol. 7 (1913), p. 724.

an English lawyer, traveller, writer, government official, and country gentleman. Sir Thomas Erskine Holland, in reviewing the work, said that "it is well planned, free from the rhetorical vagueness which has been the besetting vice of older books of a similar character, full of information, and everywhere bearing traces of the sound judgment and statesmanlike view of its author." Foreign commentators, while praising Hall's work, warn the reader against the author's national bias when questions affecting England are discussed.

Hall died in 1894, but he foresaw the ordeal of battle through which international law would be obliged to pass. In the preface to the third edition of his work, prepared in 1889, he expressed the fear that Europe was moving towards a time when international law would be severely tried. He said:

> Whole nations will be in the field; the commerce of the world may be on the sea to win or lose; national existences will be at stake; men will be tempted to do anything which will shorten hostilities and tend to a decisive answer. . . . But there can be very little doubt that if the next war is unscrupulously waged, it will also be followed by a reaction towards increased stringency of law. . . . I therefore look forward with much misgiving to the manner in which the next great war will be waged, but with no misgiving at all as to the character of the rules which will be acknowledged ten years after its termination, by comparison with the rules now considered to exist.[1]

JAMES LORIMER (1818–1890), leading Scotch writer on modern international law. His two volumes entitled *The Institutes of the Law of Nations* appeared in 1883. An abridgment in French in one volume by Ernest Nys was published in 1885. There is also a Spanish translation. Lorimer was born in Scotland in 1818 and was educated at the University of Edinburgh, then at Berlin and Bonn. He became an advocate and Regius professor of public law and of the law of nature and nations in the University of Edinburgh. He defined the law of nations as "the law of nature realized in the relations of separate nations," and he described his two volumes on this subject as "an attempt to discover the jural relations of separate political communities." He states further in his work:

> My anxiety to place international law on deeper and more stable foundations than comity or convention, and to vindicate for international jurisprudence the character of a science of nature which I have elsewhere claimed for jurisprudence as a whole, has led me to depart, to a considerable extent, from the lines which are followed in the ordinary text-books. More prominence has been given to the ethical element, and the conception of the interdependence of states has been substituted for that of their independence.[2]

FRÉDÉRIC DE MARTENS (1845–1909). De Martens was born in Estonia in 1845 and was trained as a jurist in the Ministry of Foreign

---

[1] *A Treatise on International Law* (3d ed.), pp. ix, x.
[2] *Institutes of the Law of Nations*, Vol. I (1883), Prefatory Note.

Affairs of Russia, which he entered in 1869 as counsellor and to which he was permanently attached until his death in 1909. He was also for a time professor of law in the Imperial School in St. Petersburg. He published many works, but his chief claim to fame is his treatise on international law which, published originally in the Russian language in 1883–1887, has been translated into German, French, Spanish, Japanese, Persian, Serbian, and Chinese. The fifth Russian edition appeared in 1905. De Martens represented Russia at many official conferences: the Conference of Brussels of 1874, which drew up the declaration concerning the laws of land warfare; in 1887 at the International Red Cross Conference of Carlsbad; in 1888 at the International Conference on Maritime Law, and in 1899 and 1901 at the Conference on the Abolition of the Slave Trade in Africa; in 1906 at the Conference on the Revision of the Red Cross Convention. He was instrumental in laying the foundations for the Hague Conferences of 1899 and 1907, and was a Russian delegate to both conferences, where his services were conspicuous. His reputation as an arbiter in international arbitrations earned for him the sobriquet of "Chief Justice of Christendom." Among other arbitrations in which he took part as judge, he was a member of the Hague tribunals which decided the Pious Fund Case between the United States and Mexico in 1902 and the Venezuelan Preferential Cases in 1903. During the Russo-Japanese War he was judge of the Russian Supreme Prize Court and later played an important part in the negotiations which ended that war. His treatise in French is entitled *Traité de droit international*.

PAUL PRADIER-FODÉRÉ (1827–1904). This author was born at Strasbourg in 1827 and became an advocate at Paris. In 1874, upon the commission of the Peruvian Government, he organized and for some time directed the Faculty of Political and Administrative Sciences at Lima. Upon his return to France, he was appointed counsellor at the court of Lyons. He began in 1885 the publication of a most pretentious series of volumes entitled *Traité de droit international public, européen et américain*, in which he undertook to follow the progress of the science of international law and contemporaneous practice. Volumes 1 and 2 appeared in 1885 and subsequent volumes as follows: Volume 3 (1887), Volume 4 (1888), Volume 5 (1891), Volume 6 (1894), Volume 7 (1897). Pradier-Fodéré died in 1904 and his son brought out the eighth volume in 1906, but the work is still unfinished.

MARQUIS DE OLIVART (1861–1928). This jurisconsult in the Spanish Ministry of State published in 1887–90 a work entitled *Tratado y notas de derecho internacional público*. The fourth edition in four volumes was published in 1903–4 and a supplementary volume in two parts covered the period 1903–1927.

HENRY BONFILS (1835–1897). Bonfils might be considered the first of the French writers on international law.[1] His *Manuel de droit international public* was published in 1894. Bonfils was born at Montpelier in 1835 and was professor at the Faculty of Law at Toulouse. He died in 1897, three years after the publication of his work. Paul Fauchille became the editor of subsequent editions.

PAUL FAUCHILLE (1858–1926). Fauchille revised a number of editions of Bonfils' *Manuel de droit international public*. The eighth edition, entirely rewritten and brought up to date by Fauchille, appeared as follows: Volume 2, dealing with war and neutrality, 1921; Volume 1, dealing with peace, appeared in three parts in 1922, 1925, and 1926. Fauchille was born at Lille in 1858. In 1894 he, with Antoine Pillet, founded the *Revue générale de droit international public*, and later Fauchille was one of the founders of the *Institut des Hautes Etudes Internationales*. Commenting on Fauchille's *Traité de droit international public*, which is the title under which his edition appears, Professor Wambaugh, of Harvard University, says it is "a mine of information to be searched by the specialist who has to deal with an international law problem, whether it be old or new."[2]

ALPHONSE RIVIER (1835–1898). This author was born at Lausanne in 1835. He was educated in Germany and became professor at the University of Berne in 1867. For a time he was consul general of the Swiss Confederation and later went to Brussels, where he was professor at the university. From 1867, in which year he went to Brussels, he was one of the editors of the *Revue de droit international et de législation comparée*. In 1896 he published a two-volume work entitled *Principes du droit des gens*. He had previously, in 1889, published in German a volume entitled *Lehrbuch des Völkerrechts* for the use of students. His later volumes in French, he said, were intended for publicists, diplomats, members of government and parliament, and all persons occupied with public affairs, especially with international relations. Rivier died in 1898.

ERNEST NYS (1851–1920). Nys was an active collaborator in the work of the *Institut de Droit International*. He was counsellor of the Court of Appeal at Brussels, professor at the university of that city, and a member of the Permanent Court of Arbitration. His three-volume work entitled *Le droit international; les principes, les théories, les faits*, was published in 1904–6. A new edition appeared in 1912. The work is particularly valuable for its treatment of the origin and growth of international law and historical review of the work of the authors who have successively contributed to the development of the science.

---

[1] See Nys's comment on the prior work of Sorel, *supra*, p. 39.
[2] *Am. Jour. Int. Law*, Vol. 19 (1925), p. 832.

LASSA OPPENHEIM (1858–1919). This author's treatise on *International Law*, published in 1905–6, is the outstanding modern treatise published in England. The author describes it as a work "for students written by a teacher." Oppenheim was born in Germany in 1858 and, after being educated at Göttingen, Heidelberg, Berlin, and Leipzig, he lectured in several universities in Switzerland. In 1905 he went to London, where he became lecturer on international law in the London School of Economics. From this time on he devoted himself exclusively to international law, and his treatise is regarded as the worthy successor of Hall's English treatise but, as one commentator says, free from the "deficiencies of temper, when treating of the action of nations other than the English, which disfigured the otherwise admirable volume of Hall." Oppenheim's continental training enabled him to consider properly the continental schools of international law as well as the Anglo-Saxon and to strike a balance between the two. In 1908 he succeeded John Westlake in the Whewell professorship of international law at Cambridge University, which chair he held until his death. He was joint author of the British *Manual of the Laws and Usages of War on Land*. Several new editions of his treatise on international law have appeared under the editorship of others, the last being the fifth edition in 1935 by Dr. H. Lauterpacht.

CHAPTER IV

CUSTOM AS A SOURCE OF INTERNATIONAL LAW

From a previous chapter we have seen that the obligations of natural law exist independently of the consent of men, and by analogy it is reasoned that the principles of the natural law are binding upon nations also independently of their consent. James Kent, an early commentator on American law, expressed the idea thus: "States, or bodies politic, are to be considered as moral persons, having a public will, capable and free to do right and wrong, inasmuch as they are collections of individuals, each of whom carries with him into the service of the community the same binding law of morality and religion which ought to control his conduct in private life." [1] If we admit the analogy of the possession of natural rights by states as well as by men, it is a necessary corollary that the state, like the individual, is under the necessity of instituting means to secure its natural rights. The Declaration of Independence of the United States starts with the premise that man is endowed with certain inalienable rights and then declares that to secure these rights governments are instituted among men. The same should be true in a world made up of a number of separate and independent states, each possessing what it claims to be certain natural rights. To secure these natural rights of the states, it seems necessary that they be protected by a positive legal order as the natural rights of the individual are safeguarded within the state.

This leads to the consideration of the next great source of international law, namely, that law which is based upon the consent of nations. Consent may be tacitly expressed by long usage, practice, and custom, or explicitly expressed by being embodied in conventions or treaties. Of these sources, custom is the oldest not only as a source of international law in particular but of law in general. It has as its guarantee the consensus of opinion and usage of the civilized world, and it forms intrinsically the most important portion of international law, for it is deeply rooted in the habits, sentiments, and interests of mankind.[2]

The discussion of custom as a source of international law brings up at the outset the consideration of the Austinian theory of law as proceeding from a supreme lawgiver, for obviously a theory under which law has resulted from the long-continued usages of individuals acting uniformly in a given set of circumstances cannot be consistent with another theory which insists that the law is promulgated by a superior

[1] Kent, *Commentaries on American Law* (1826), Vol. I, pp. 3-4.
[2] Hershey, *Essentials of International Public Law and Organization* (1927), p. 24.

44

authority who invokes penalties for the violation of his commands. This conflict in theory is not peculiar to international law. It exists as well in municipal law, but is not so pronounced there because of the more advanced development of legal systems supported by political institutions. Let us therefore approach the subject from the broad point of view of law in general.

We are told by Dr. Thomas A. Walker, of Cambridge, who died only a few years ago and whose volume on the *Science of International Law*, published in 1893, is one of the most valuable treatises in the English language, that "early law is not command enunciated by a determinate sovereign legislator, and guarded by regular penalties of fine or corporal punishment, but custom administered by some headman, priest, patriarch, princeps or popular magistrate, and sanctioned by social ostracism, descended, perhaps, from a still earlier devotion to the infernal gods, and descending into practical downright outlawry, the fixing of the wolf's head. Custom," he says, "precedes proper law in the beginning of states, and not infrequently extends its sway far among the facts of modern political organization. For," he continues,

when we examine primitive associations larger than the family, and popular society as advanced in political life as were the Germans of Tacitus, we find nothing of the character of Austinian "Law": we find rulers, but these rulers are not legislators but judges; we find councils of elders, but these again are not lawmakers, but assessors, advisers of the headman or the monarch; we find popular assemblies, but these are not legislative parliaments, but the meetings of the host, the meetings of the whole free people in arms for deliberation as to some external movement, or for the supervision of the customary land distribution.

Consequently, it is held that primitive law is custom, custom observed on account of its antiquity or on account of its supposed divine origin. It is enforced not by the use of the axe or the scimitar, the knout or the bayonet, but by the public opinion of the community. "The truth is," Walker says, "that the opinion of an indeterminate body is often a sanction far more effective than are the penalties annexed by the determinate legislator. In the most strongly centralized community the success or failure of a legislative measure will depend upon the fact that it is, or is not, a reflection of current popular opinion." Therefore, he concludes that custom is complete law in itself, its own legislator, and its own sanction.[1]

We agree that a specific sanction is not an indispensable element of true law, however necessary such means of enforcement may be in certain kinds of legislation miscalled law. The millions of honest, peaceful people who belong to and constitute the separate states of the world are law-abiding not because they do not wish to feel the con-

[1] Walker, *The Science of International Law* (1893), Chap. I, Sec. 1.

straint of the civil process server or because they fear the penalties of the criminal law; they obey the law because they believe in it and prefer to observe it.   This truism was pointed out in the very first article which appeared in the first number of the *American Journal of International Law*, in January, 1907, by the Honorable Elihu Root, the first president of the American Society of International Law, and now America's eldest statesman.[1]   In pointing out the need of popular understanding of international law, Mr. Root remarked:

In every civil community it is necessary to have courts to determine rights and officers to compel observance of the law; yet the true basis of the peace and order in which we live is not fear of the policeman; it is the self-restraint of the thousands of people who make up the community and their willingness to obey the law and regard the rights of others.   The true basis of business is not the sheriff with a writ of execution; it is the voluntary observance of the rules and obligations of business life which are universally recognized as essential to business success.

Nor does the violation of law, or even the failure to inflict punishment for the violation, abrogate the law or prove its non-existence. These propositions are accepted as axiomatic in the realm of municipal law.   They must therefore also be true in the domain of international law whose evolution can be regarded as now paralleling an earlier stage in the slow processes by which municipal law has advanced from complete reliance upon self-help to the present highly organized legal order in which self-help is recognized as legitimate only in cases of self-defense.

The question of the sanction of international law arose in a case decided in 1906 in the Supreme Court of Hongkong.   A Norwegian steamship, the *Prometheus*, was leased to a Japanese steamship company on condition that it would not be used for the transportation of contraband of war, Japan then being at war with Russia.   A dispute over this condition arose and the construction of the terms of the charter-party was submitted to the Chief Justice of Hongkong.   He stated the question and decided it as follows:

It was contended on behalf of the owners of the Prometheus that the term "law" as applied to this recognized system of principles and rules known as international law is an inexact expression, that there is, in other words, no such thing as international law; that there can be no such law binding upon all nations inasmuch as there is no sanction for such law, that is to say that there is no means by which obedience to such law can be imposed upon any given nation refusing obedience thereto.   I do not concur in that contention.   In my opinion a law may be established and become international law, that is to say binding upon all nations, by the agreement of such nations to be bound thereby, although it may be impossible to enforce obedience thereto by any given nation party to the agreement.   The resistance of a nation to a law to which it has agreed does not derogate from the authority of the law because that resistance cannot, perhaps, be overcome.   Such resistance merely makes the resisting nation a breaker of the

[1] Mr. Root died February 7, 1937.

law to which it has given its adherence, but it leaves the law, to the establishment of which the resisting nation was a party, still subsisting. Could it be successfully contended that because any given person or body of persons possessed for the time being power to resist an established municipal law such law had no existence? The answer to such a contention would be that the law still existed, though it might not for the time being be possible to enforce obedience to it.[1]

This judicial statement disposes, at least to our satisfaction, of the objection to international law, whether customary or conventional, based upon the alleged lack of a sanction to enforce it, and we return to our immediate topic of custom as a source of international law.

The terms "custom" and "usage" are used synonymously in everyday life and language, but to the jurist they have two distinctly different meanings, and in legal terminology custom should not be confounded with usage. Jurists speak of a custom when a continuous habit of doing certain actions has grown up under the conviction that such actions are legally necessary or legally right. On the other hand, jurists speak of a usage when a habit of doing certain things develops without involving any conviction of their legal character. Thus the term "custom" in legal language is a narrower conception than the term "usage," as a given course of conduct may be usual without being customary. Therefore, the conduct of states concerning certain of their international relations may be usual but not predicated upon customary international law.[2]

Usages have a tendency to become customs, and the question is presented, at what time does a usage become a custom? The question is one of fact. A simple illustration of the growth of usage and its development into custom is given by Pitt Cobbett, who likens the process to the formation of a path across a common. "At first," he says, "each wayfarer pursues his own course; gradually, by reason either of its directness or on some other ground of apparent utility, some particular route is followed by the majority; this route next assumes the character of a track, discernible but not as yet well defined, from which deviation, however, now becomes more rare; whilst in its final stage the route assumes the shape of a well-defined path, habitually followed by all who pass that way. And yet it would be difficult to point out at what precise moment this route acquired the character of an acknowledged path." The growth of usage and formation of custom proceeds much on the same lines both in a community of individuals and in the community of nations. To quote Pitt Cobbett again:

As between nations some particular practice or course of conduct arises, attributable in the first instance to some particular emergency or prompted by a

[1] 2 Hongkong Law Reports, 207; Dickinson, *Cases on the Law of Nations* (1929), p. 33; Fenwick, *Cases on International Law* (1935), p. 21; Scott, *Cases on International Law* (1922), pp. 967–8.
[2] Oppenheim, *International Law* (2d ed.), Vol. I, p. 21.

common belief in its convenience or safety.   But its observance is discretionary; and it exists side by side with other competing practices.   Next, as between com-peting usages the fittest, having regard to the needs of the time generally tends to prevail.   It gathers strength by observance.   It comes to be recorded, and is appealed to in cases of dispute, although not infrequently violated.   Finally, it comes to command a general assent; and at this stage it may be said to take on the character of a custom, which involves not merely a habit of action, but a rule of conduct resting on general approval.[1]

The next question which presents itself for answer is, How may it be determined what constitutes an authoritative international custom? As Hall points out, up to a certain point there is no difficulty in answer-ing this question.   "A large part of international usage gives effect to principles which represent facts of state existence, essential under the conditions of modern civilized state life. . . . The assumption that they are essential, so far as that group of states which is subject to inter-national law is concerned, lies at the root of the whole of civilized inter-national conduct; and that they have come to be regarded in this light, and unquestionably continue to be so regarded, is sufficient reason for taking as authoritative the principles and rules which result from them."[2]

By way of example, we might cite such fundamental principles as the right of every nation to continued existence, to independence, to ex-clusive jurisdiction over its own territory, and to legal equality with every other nation.   Such fundamental principles were the subject of a declaration adopted by the American Institute of International Law at its inaugural session in Washington, January 6, 1916.[3]   Commenting upon this Declaration of the Rights and Duties of Nations, Mr. Elihu Root observed:

These are the fundamentals of international right.   They involve the existence of a democratic community of nations in which each individual nation has the same rights and full liberty for their enjoyment, limited and limited only, by the equal rights of every other member of the community.   The body of rules of action which long experience and general consent have worked out for the asser-tion and preservation of these rights and the application of the universal limita-tion upon them in the practical relations between nations constitutes interna-tional law.[4]

When a general rule of customary international law is invoked against a state, it is not necessary that the state in question shall have as-sented to the rule either diplomatically or by having acted on it.   It is enough to show that the general consensus of opinion within the limits of civilization is in favor of the rule.[5]

[1] Cobbett, *Cases and Opinions on International Law* (3d ed., 1909), Pt. I, pp. 5–6.
[2] *International Law* (1880), p. 5.
[3] *Am. Jour. Int. Law*, Vol. 10 (1916), pp. 121–6.
[4] *Proceedings of the American Society of International Law*, 1916, p. 4.
[5] Westlake, *International Law*, Pt. I (1910), p. 16.

Every state has a right to presume the continuance of customs which have long subsisted between nations: they are rarely to be departed from, and then only after due notice conveyed to other countries, and only in those cases in which it may be competent for a nation so to act. For instance, the privileges and immunities of a foreign ambassador are secured to him by the universal custom of all nations which it is not competent for any individual nation at its pleasure to abrogate or deny.

When in 1708 the Ambassador of Peter the Great in London was arrested in an action for debt and compelled to give bail, the Czar demanded his liberation and an apology, and in these demands Russia was joined by the ambassadors and ministers of the other nations. The persons concerned in the arrest were prosecuted by the Attorney General, and after examination before the Privy Council, seventeen were committed to prison. To appease the indignation of the Czar, Parliament passed the famous Statute of Anne (7 Anne 12), which declared void all the proceedings against the Russian Ambassador and provided severe penalties for future violations of diplomatic immunities. An illuminated copy of the statute was sent to the Czar by special ambassador.[1] The Statute of Anne was adopted in substantially the same terms by the United States Congress in 1790 and incorporated in the Revised Statutes of the United States (R.S. 4063–4064). Lord Mansfield, in the later case of Triquet v. Bath (1764), said that the statute was merely declaratory of the law of nations.[2]

A modern incident occurred when the German Minister was killed by the Boxers in Peking in 1900. The Chinese Government made full apologies by a special mission sent to Germany, and was required to punish the murderers, and to erect a monument to the dead foreign diplomat. All other powers whose diplomatic representatives were besieged in the legation quarter in Peking required China to visit condign punishment upon the guilty leaders who could be taxed with criminal responsibility for the acts of the Boxers, and exacted indemnities for the cost of sending their armies to the relief of their representatives whose lives were threatened by the uprising in the capital of China.[3]

Diplomatic incidents involving other branches of the law also illustrate the rule that states may not depart from established custom, at least without protest more often effective than not.

During the American Civil War a cruiser of the United States stopped an English mail packet, the Trent, plying between neutral ports, and

[1] Case of Mattueof (1709), 88 Eng. Rep. 598; Evans, Cases on International Law (1922), p. 229, note.
[2] 3 Burr. 1478; Dickinson, Cases on the Law of Nations (1929), p. 55; Fenwick, Cases on International Law (1935), p. 31; Scott, Cases on International Law (1922), p. 2.
[3] See Foreign Relations of the United States, 1901, Appendix: Affairs in China.

forcibly removed therefrom two representatives of the Southern Confederacy, not in its military service, bound for England. England promptly demanded the release of these persons, and to this demand were added the protests of France, Prussia, and Austria. The demand and protests were based upon the assertion that under the circumstances the neutral flag completely covered the persons and cargo on board the neutral vessel; that the action of the American commander constituted an interference with neutral rights on the sea, the legality of which was not admitted under the rules of modern international law; and that approval could not be given to this isolated act of the United States without infringing upon the existing rights of all neutrals.[1] The Government of the United States decided that the captain of the American cruiser had acted without instructions and surrendered the prisoners to Great Britain.

In its turn, the United States became the champion of neutral rights and objected to similar action by France and Great Britain during the war in 1915. A German waiter employed on the American vessel *Windber* from Colon, Panama Canal Zone, to New York, was seized on the high seas by officers of a French cruiser, and taken to Jamaica, where he was detained as a prisoner by the British authorities. The United States promptly protested to both France and Great Britain and demanded the prisoner's release, citing the principles relied upon by those governments in the *Trent* affair. After several months of diplomatic correspondence, he was liberated.[2]

Besides the rules of international law which are universally binding upon all civilized states, there are other rules which may be binding upon a large number but less than the entire body of states, and still other rules which bind only two or a few states only. In cases involving rules of international law whose acceptance is less than universal, how may the consent of any given state be proved?

This question came before the Court of King's Bench of England in 1905, in the case of West Rand Central Gold Ming Co. v. The King,[3] in which Lord Robert Cecil, arguing that all contractual obligations incurred by a conquered state before war breaks out pass upon annexation to the conqueror, relied upon the proposition that international law forms part of the law of England. Commenting upon this broad assertion, Lord Chief Justice Alverstone said:

[1] Bernard, *The Neutrality of Great Britain during the American Civil War* (1870), pp. 196–200. English translation of the notes of Austria, France, and Prussia are printed in the *Am. Jour. Int. Law*, Supp., Vol. 10 (1916), pp. 67–72. See the address of Honorable Elihu Root before the American Society of International Law, April 27, 1916, *Proceedings*, p. 8.

[2] See correspondence in *Am. Jour. Int. Law*, Spl. Supp., Vol. 9 (1915), pp. 353–60.

[3] L. R. [1905] 2 K. B. 391; Dickinson, *Cases on the Law of Nations* (1929), pp. 62, 943; Fenwick, *Cases on International Law* (1935), pp. 33, 105; Hudson, *Cases on International Law* (1936), p. 723; Scott, *Cases on International Law* (1922), pp. 7–8.

It is quite true that whatever has received the common consent of civilized nations must have received the assent of our country, and that to which we have assented along with other nations in general may properly be called international law, and as such will be acknowledged and applied by our municipal tribunals when legitimate occasion arises for those tribunals to decide questions to which doctrines of international law may be relevant. But any doctrine so invoked must be one really accepted as binding between nations, and the international law sought to be applied must, like anything else, be proved by satisfactory evidence, which must shew either that the particular proposition put forward has been recognized and acted upon by our country, or that it is of such a nature, and has been so widely and generally accepted, that it can hardly be supposed that any civilized state would repudiate it. The mere opinions of jurists, however eminent or learned, that it ought to be so recognized, are not in themselves sufficient. They must have received the express sanction of international agreement, or gradually have grown to be part of international law by their frequent practical recognition in dealings between various nations.

Adverting to an expression by Lord Mansfield in the case of Triquet *v.* Bath, previously cited, that the law of nations forms part of the law of England, Chief Justice Alverstone pointed out that Lord Mansfield was dealing with an established rule of international law which recognizes the privileges of ambassadors. Such an expression, he held, ought not to be construed so as to include a question as to which there is no evidence that Great Britain has ever assented.[1]

The evidence of the consent of states to particular rules of international law is furnished by their actions, in their treaties with other states, in their national law and ordinances, in the decisions of their courts, in their state papers and diplomatic correspondence; in fact, "every written document, every record of act or spoken word which presents an authentic picture of the practice of states in their international dealings."[2] Consequently, one who would expound international law must be versed in history and familiar with historical methods.

The original repository of most of the documentary material evidencing the practice of states is usually the archives of foreign offices; but unfortunately such archives are too often either closed to public inspection or their contents are otherwise not easily accessible. When-

---

[1] In the case of the *Paquete Habana* (1900), 175 U. S. 677, the Supreme Court of the United States held that "International law is part of our law, and must be ascertained and administered by the courts of justice of appropriate jurisdiction, as often as questions of right depending upon it are duly presented for their determination."

The Constitution of the United States confers upon Congress the power "to define and punish . . . offenses against the law of nations." Provisions declaring that international law forms a part of the law of the country are also found in several modern constitutions, including: Venezuela (1904), Germany, Austria and Estonia (1920), and Spain (1931).

For a discussion of the theory of the incorporation of international law into municipal law, see article by Prof. E. D. Dickinson entitled "Changing Concepts and the Doctrine of Incorporation," *Am. Jour. Int. Law*, Vol. 26 (1932), p. 239.

[2] Walker, *History of the Law of Nations* (1899), Vol. I, Chap. 2.

ever material of this character is made available, it constitutes primary evidence of the attitude of the state whose document is cited toward the particular rule of international law which may be in question. Sir Ernest Satow gives a valuable summary of the archives on foreign affairs available in European countries.[1] Such published series as *British and Foreign State Papers* and *Foreign Relations of the United States* are helpful, although not always satisfactory because of the incompleteness of the material included.

Of greater value as repositories of international law are collections such as the *Digest of International Law*, edited by John Bassett Moore and published by the United States Government in 1906. This monumental eight-volume work is described as containing international law embodied in diplomatic discussions, treaties and other international agreements, international awards, the decisions of municipal courts, and the writings of jurists, and especially any documents, published and unpublished, issued by presidents and secretaries of state of the United States, the opinions of the attorneys-general, and the decisions of courts, federal and state. In his preface to this work, Judge Moore warns the reader that "mere extracts from state papers or judicial decisions can not be safely relied on as guides to the law. They may indeed be positively misleading. Especially is this true of state papers, in which arguments are often contentiously put forth which by no means represent the eventual view of the government in whose behalf they were employed." Besides quoting particular documents, Judge Moore gives the history of each case, presents the views of both sides and, by showing what was finally done, "discloses the opinion that in the end prevailed."

Unilateral state documents at times mark the adoption of important national policies which, being later approved and followed by other states, eventually ripen into general international law. Of such a character was the neutrality proclamation of President Washington of April 22, 1793, and the neutrality law enacted by the Congress of the United States upon the President's recommendation and approved June 5, 1794. The effect of the law and policy of the United States of that period upon the subsequent development of the permanent law of neutrality throughout the world has been recorded by the English writer Hall, who said:

The policy of the United States in 1793 constitutes an epoch in the development of the usages of neutrality. There can be no doubt that it was intended and believed to give effect to the obligations then incumbent upon neutrals. But it represented by far the most advanced existing opinions as to what those obligations were; and in some points it even went further than authoritative interna-

[1] *Guide to Diplomatic Practice* (2d ed.), Vol. I, pp. 13–21.

tional custom has up to the present time advanced. In the main however it is identical with the standard of conduct which is now adopted by the community of nations.[1]

Sometimes special authority is claimed for the practice of those states which are most concerned with a particular branch of international law. While there may be good foundation for such a claim in the fact that the powers most concerned with a subject must understand it best, on the other hand, special knowledge is often accompanied by the bias of special interest. "But," says Westlake, "when the states most concerned with a subject in turn apply the same rules and suffer their application, that bias may be supposed to be eliminated, and the agreement which those concerned in the vast majority of cases find suitable must count for a general agreement in spite of much comparatively speculative criticism from other quarters." [2]

The decisions of the prize courts of great maritime powers may be mentioned to illustrate the point which Mr. Westlake thus makes. Owing to the preponderance of the interests of these powers, the decisions of their courts on questions of maritime law carry much weight. Consequently, a few cases arising in British and American courts will be cited by way of demonstrating the growth of customary international law.

The first case to be mentioned involved the question of the locality of the forum in the matter of jurisdiction to condemn a prize. The *Flad Oyen*, an English ship, was captured in 1798 by a French privateer and taken to Bergen, Norway, that country being neutral. The English ship was condemned as prize by the French Consul at Bergen and sold to a Danish merchant. On a subsequent voyage out of Bergen the ship was retaken by the British, and the Danish purchaser at Bergen claimed the *Flad Oyen* as his property. Lord Stowell, then Sir William Scott, speaking for the High Court of Admiralty, after pointing out that prize courts act and exercise their functions in the belligerent country, stated with reference to the case at bar, "it is for the very first time in the world, that in the year 1799, an attempt is made to impose upon the court a sentence of a tribunal not existing in the belligerent country, but of a person pretending to be authorized within the dominions of a neutral country." Even if it could be shown, he said, that such a condemnation ought to be deemed sufficient on general principles, that would not be enough, for, "it must be shown that it is conformable to the usage and practice of nations." Speaking in general terms, Lord Stowell continued:

A great part of the law of nations stands on no other foundation; it is introduced, indeed, by general principles, but it travels with those principles only to a

---

[1] Hall, *International Law* (3d ed.), p. 594.
[2] Westlake, *International Law* (1910), Pt. I, p. 17.

certain extent; and, if it stops there, you are not at liberty to go farther, and to say, that mere general speculations would bear you out in a further progress. Thus, for instance, on mere general principles it is lawful to destroy your enemy, and mere general principles make no great difference as to the manner by which this is to be effected; but the conventional law of mankind, which is evidenced in their practice, does make a distinction, and allows some, and prohibits other modes of destruction; and a belligerent is bound to confine himself to those modes which the common practice of mankind has employed, and to relinquish those which the same practice has not brought within the ordinary exercise of war, however sanctioned by its principles and purposes.

Turning to the case before him, Lord Stowell held:

Now, it having been the constant usage, that the tribunals of the law of nations in these matters shall exercise their functions within the belligerent country; if it was proved to me in the clearest manner, that on mere general theory such a tribunal might act in the neutral country, I must take my stand on the ancient and universal practice of mankind, and say that as far as that practice has gone, I am willing to go, and where it has thought proper to stop, there I must stop likewise.

It is my duty not to admit, that because one nation has thought proper to depart from the common usage of the world, and to meet the notice of mankind in a new and unprecedented manner, that I am on that account under the necessity of acknowledging the efficacy of such a novel institution, merely because general theory might give it a degree of countenance, independent of all practice from the earliest history of mankind. The institution must conform to the text law, and likewise to the constant usage of the matter; and when I am told, that before the present war, no sentence of this kind has ever been produced in the annals of mankind, and that it is produced by one nation only in this war, I require nothing more to satisfy me, that it is the duty of this court to reject such a sentence as inadmissible.[1]

We have already seen that the beginnings of the law of the sea are to be found in the ancient sea codes dating to the early centuries of the Christian era and spreading in subsequent centuries throughout the maritime world. A comparatively recent case, the argument of which spanned the centuries from the days of the ancient codes, shows the working of the same processes in the formation of the modern law of the sea. In 1863, with the advent of steam navigation, the British Government adopted a series of regulations for preventing collisions at sea. Practically the same regulations were adopted by the United States Congress in 1864, and within a short time thereafter many other maritime countries indicated their willingness that the British regulations should apply to their ships when outside British jurisdiction. Subsequently, a British steamer named the *Scotia* collided in mid-ocean with an American sailing ship, the *Berkshire*, which was sunk. The owners of the *Berkshire* alleged in a libel filed in the United States

[1] (1799) 1 C. Rob. 135; Hudson, *Cases on International Law* (1936), p. 1395; Scott, *Cases on International Law* (1922), p. 1070.

District Court in New York that the collision occurred through the fault of the *Scotia*, arguing that the vessels at the time of the collision were governed by the general maritime law as it existed before the British legislation of 1863. On appeal to the Supreme Court of the United States, Mr. Justice Strong, who delivered the opinion of the court, replied to the question, what was the law of the place where and at the time the collision occurred, as follows:

Conceding that it was not the law of the United States, nor that of Great Britain, nor the concurrent regulations of the two governments, but that it was the law of the sea, was it the ancient maritime law, that which existed before the commercial nations of the world adopted the regulations of 1863 and 1864, or the law changed after those regulations were adopted? Undoubtedly, no single nation can change the law of the sea. That law is of universal obligation, and no statute of one or two nations can create obligations for the world. Like all the laws of nations, it rests upon the common consent of civilized communities. It is of force, not because it was prescribed by any superior power, but because it has been generally accepted as a rule of conduct. Whatever may have been its origin, whether in the usages of navigation or in the ordinances of maritime states, or in both, it has become the law of the sea only by the concurrent sanction of those nations who may be said to constitute the commercial world. Many of the usages which prevail, and which have the force of law, doubtless originated in the positive prescriptions of some single state, which were at first of limited effect, but which when generally accepted became of universal obligation. The Rhodian law is supposed to have been the earliest system of marine rules. It was a code for Rhodians only, but it soon became of general authority because accepted and assented to as a wise and desirable system by other maritime nations. The same may be said of the Amalphitan table, of the ordinances of the Hanseatic League, and of parts of the marine ordinances of Louis XIV. They all became the law of the sea, not on account of their origin, but by reason of their acceptance as such.

In these sentences, the Supreme Court of the United States placed the *imprimatur* of its high judicial authority upon the concept of law emanating from continuous usage implying general consent as opposed to the concept of law imposed by a superior authority, and the court invoked the doctrine so approved to define the nature and authority of the customary law of nations. This method of finding and declaring the law the court held to be indispensable, for "unless general assent is efficacious to give sanction to international law," the law cannot develop to meet constant changes and necessities.

Applying these principles to the case before the court, the decision proceeded as follows:

Changes in nautical rules have taken place. How have they been accomplished, if not by the concurrent assent, express or understood, of maritime nations? When, therefore, we find such rules of navigation as are mentioned in the British orders in council of January 9th, 1863, and in our act of Congress of 1864, accepted as obligatory rules by more than thirty of the principal commercial states of the world, including almost all which have any shipping on the Atlantic Ocean, we are constrained to regard them as in part at least, and so far as relates to these vessels, the laws of the sea, and as having been the law at the time when the collision of which the libellants complain took place.

This is not giving to the statutes of any nation extraterritorial effect. It is not treating them as general maritime laws, but it is recognition of the historical fact that, by common consent of mankind, these rules have been acquiesced in as of general obligation. Of that fact we think we may take judicial notice. Foreign municipal laws must indeed be proved as facts, but it is not so with the law of nations.[1]

In consequence of this ruling, the court held that the *Berkshire* and not the *Scotia* was at fault.

Another factor in the growth of international law which should be considered in connection with custom is the so-called Comity of Nations. This term is explained by Oppenheim as follows: "In their intercourse with one another, states do observe not only legally binding rules and such rules as have the character of usages, but also rules of politeness, convenience and good will. Such rules of international conduct are not rules of law, but of comity." [2] The international law of the present day owes much to the comity of nations as a source from which its rules were derived. A few examples will serve to illustrate the process of evolution.

First, an example taken from diplomatic practice. The continuous residence of an embassy was originally a matter of comity, but the practice long ago developed into custom, which is now so universally recognized that the obligation to maintain diplomatic intercourse with foreign states is held to be a legal duty.[3] The forcing upon China and Japan of diplomatic and commercial intercourse by the Western powers in the middle of the nineteenth century leaves no doubt at the present time of the binding nature of this obligation.

Secondly, an illustration showing the transition from usage based on comity to law based on formal agreement by treaty. Such a transformation is now taking place in the matter of international extradition. The demand upon a state to deliver up a person accused of the commission of a crime in another has often conflicted with the right claimed by the latter state to grant asylum to fugitives from other countries. Furthermore, states have assumed the position that the enforcement of the penal law of other states was no concern of theirs. No obligation to extradite is therefore imposed by the law or usage of nations. In the absence of treaty, compliance with a demand for extradition rests

[1] 14 Wallace, 170; Dickinson, *Cases on the Law of Nations* (1929), p. 29; Fenwick, *Cases on International Law* (1935), p. 18; Hudson, *Cases on International Law* (1936), p. 667. [2] *International Law* (2d ed.), Vol. I, p. 24.
[3] Satow, *Diplomatic Practice* (2d ed.), Vol. I, p. 195; Hyde, *International Law Chiefly as Interpreted and Applied by the United States* (1922), Vol. I, p. 90.

upon comity or convenience; but the world-wide intercourse between nations and their nationals in recent years resulting from improvement in the means of transportation and communication has made international coöperation in the suppression of crime highly expedient, if not absolutely necessary, and bilateral treaties making extradition an obligation of international conventional law have been concluded with increasing frequency. To make this conventional law more effective and eliminate conflicts in divergent practices of states, it has latterly been officially recommended that certain questions connected with extradition are susceptible of being dealt with in a general international convention.[1] No further official action has been taken, but the Research in International Law under the auspices of the Faculty of Harvard Law School has recently drawn up a draft convention on the subject of extradition,[2] with the advice and collaboration of a group of about fifty outstanding members of the American Bar and teaching profession.

Lastly, we have a judicial record of the transition of a usage based upon the comity of nations into a legal obligation of customary international law. Under the general rule, enemy private property on the high seas is subject to capture; but an exception exists in favor of small fishing boats engaged in their legitimate pursuits. This exemption is said to date back at least to 1403.[3] During the Spanish American War of 1898, two small Spanish fishing smacks were captured at sea by United States gunboats. They were libelled in a prize court and condemned as enemy property. On appeal to the Supreme Court, it was ordered that the proceeds of the sale of the vessels and cargoes be restored to the Spanish owners with damages and costs. On behalf of the captors, there was cited the judgment of Lord Stowell in the case of the *Young Jacob and Johanna*, a small Dutch fishing vessel captured in 1798 on her return from the Dogger Bank to Holland. In upholding that capture, Lord Stowell stated that the exemption of small fishing vessels from capture in former wars "was a rule of comity only, and not of legal decision; it has prevailed from views of mutual accommodation between neighboring countries, and from tenderness to a poor and industrious people."[4] But the Supreme Court of the United States, after reviewing numerous text-writers from the important maritime countries and citing the practice of nations during the wars of the intervening one hundred years since Lord Stowell's judgment, held that:

---

[1] Report on Extradition, League of Nations Committee of Experts for the Progressive Codification of International Law, January, 1926. League of Nations Document, C.51.M.28.1926.V.; *Am. Jour. Int. Law*, Spl. Supp., Vol. 26 (1920), p. 242.

[2] The draft convention, with extended comment and relevant documents, is printed in the Supplement to the *Am. Jour. Int. Law* for April, 1935 (Vol. 29, Nos. 1 and 2).

[3] Taylor, *International Public Law* (1901), pp. 252–3.

[4] 1 C. Rob. 20; Scott, *Cases on International Law* (1922), p. 17.

This review of the precedents and authorities on the subject appears to us abundantly to demonstrate that at the present day, by the general consent of the civilized nations of the world, and independently of any express treaty or other public act, it is an established rule of international law, founded on considerations of humanity to a poor and industrious order of men, and of the mutual convenience of belligerent states, that coast fishing vessels, with their implements and supplies, cargoes and crews, unarmed and honestly pursuing their peaceful calling of catching and bringing in fresh fish, are exempt from capture as prize of war. . . . This rule of international law is one which prize courts, administering the law of nations, are bound to take judicial notice of, and to give effect to, in the absence of any treaty or other public act of their own government in relation to the matter.[1]

[1] *The Paquete Habana* (1900), 175 U. S. 677; Dickinson, *Cases on the Law of Nations.* (1929), p. 44; Fenwick, *Cases on International Law* (1935), p. 17; Scott, *Cases on International Law* (1922), p. 15.

CHAPTER V

TREATIES AS A SOURCE OF INTERNATIONAL LAW

International law based upon the consent of nations consists, we have seen, of two main divisions—the law tacitly consented to, which has been discussed under the heading of customary law, and international law explicitly accepted in documentary form such as treaties and conventions, which is the subject of the present discourse.

Treaties constitute a source of international law by reason of the lack of development in international relations of agencies analogous to the law-enacting and law-determining branches in the internal constitutional structure of states. Wheaton, writing in 1846, says: "While in every civil society or state there is always a legislative power which establishes, by express declaration, the civil law of that state, and a judicial power, which interprets that law, and applies it to individual cases, in the great society of nations there is no legislative power, and consequently there are no express laws, except those which result from the conventions which states may make with one another." [1]

Oppenheim, writing in the twentieth century, emphasizes the point by stating that "the only way in which international law can be made by a deliberate act, in contradistinction to custom, is that the members of the family of nations conclude treaties in which certain rules for their future conduct are stipulated." [2]

In a legislative body laws are usually enacted by a majority vote of the members, or by a number of votes less than the entire membership. Unanimity is never required. But till now there has been no such thing in the international community as rule by the majority. States are bound only by such international conventions or other acts as they choose to agree to by signature and ratification or by other recognized methods of signifying acceptance. Thus the general practice of international conferences requires unanimous agreement for the adoption of an international act intended to bind all the members.

It would obviously be futile to rest international law upon those treaties only which have been unanimously accepted; and the same thing may be said of customary international law. There is on this point an organic weakness in the theories of those super-Positivists who insist first, that all international law must be based upon the con-

[1] Henry Wheaton, *Elements of International Law* (3d ed., 1846), p. 3.
[2] Oppenheim, *International Law* (2d ed.), Vol. I, p. 23.

sent of states and, secondly, that the consent must be that of the whole community of states.   It may well be that the fundamental principles of international law are so universally recognized as to be regarded as being based upon the consent of all states, but, as we have previously pointed out, those fundamental principles bind states even without their explicit consent.   Such principles are rarely, if ever, the subject of express international stipulations.   To restrict the scope of international law to the rules or principles to which all nations have expressly assented would reduce the system almost to the vanishing point.   This result was pointed out nearly a century and a half ago by George Frederick de Martens, professor of law in the University of Göttingen, who in 1789 wrote: "On the example of two nations, all the nations of Europe might, by common consent, make treaties to regulate their different rights; and, then, these general treaties would form a code, which might be called the positive law of nations.   But there never yet existed such a general treaty, neither between all the powers of Europe, nor even between the majority of them; in this sense, then, there exists no positive law of nations, and, perhaps, none such ever will exist." [1] De Martens understood perfectly well that "what is become a law between two or three, or even the majority, of the powers of Europe, either by treaty or from custom, can produce neither rights nor obligations among the others."   But what we conceive to be the true scope of international law as it has been understood and practiced from the earliest known beginnings of the science up to the present time was stated by De Martens in the following paragraph:

However, by comparing the treaties that the powers of Europe have made with one another, we discover certain principles, that have been almost universally adopted by all the powers that have made treaties on the same subject.   It is the same with respect to custom: a custom received among the majority of the powers of Europe, particularly among the great powers (when it is not founded upon their particular constitutions), is easily adopted by other powers, as far as it can apply to them; and, in general, all nations give a certain degree of attention to the customs admitted by others, although it cannot be proved, that they have ever been admitted by themselves.   It is true, we cannot say as much of express conventions; it, nevertheless, often happens, that a treaty, made with such or such a power, serves as a model for the treaties of the same sort, to be made with other powers; and, very often, what takes place in one nation in virtue of treaty, is admitted in others as a custom; so that, in many points, the law of nations is founded on treaty in one country and on custom in another.

De Martens' definition of the positive law of nations was accordingly "the aggregate of the rights and obligations established among the nations of Europe (or the majority of them), whether by particular

[1] *Précis du droit des gens moderne de l'Europe, fondé sur les traités et l'usage* (Göttingen, 1789), Vol. I, pp. 3–4.

but uniform treaties, by tacit convention, or by custom, which form the general positive law of nations." [1]

The content of international law as thus expounded by De Martens is reiterated by many modern writers. Oppenheim, who writes with the precision so helpful to the student, says that "law-making treaties create law for the contracting parties solely. Their law is universal international law then only when all the members of the family of nations are parties to them." As for law-making treaties concluded by a few states only, Oppenheim says that "the law which they create is particular international law"; and besides universal and particular international law, Oppenheim classifies as general international law the body of principles included within the paragraph from De Martens above set out. In this class Oppenheim places law-making treaties containing general international law which have been concluded by the majority of states, including the leading powers. Such general international law has a tendency to become universal because, as Oppenheim explains, "such states as heretofore did not consent to it will in future either expressly give their consent or recognize the respective rules tacitly through custom."

An example which illustrates both De Martens' statement that the law of nations may be founded on treaty in one country and on custom in another and Oppenheim's reference to general international law becoming universal is provided by the Declaration of Paris of 1856 dealing with the law of war on the sea. Among the governments which declined to accede to that declaration at the time it was drawn up was the United States, and Spain had made a reservation to the declaration on the subject of privateering, but when these two countries were at war in 1898, both, without mentioning the declaration by name, agreed to abide by its rules, the United States referring to them as "recognized rules of international law." [2]

It would be erroneous to attempt to draw too sharply the line of distinction between custom and treaty as sources of international law, for, as again pointed out by Oppenheim, "it must be emphasized that, whereas custom is the original source of international law, treaties are a source the power of which derives from custom. For the fact that treaties can stipulate rules of international conduct at all is based

[1] G. F. de Martens, *Summary of the Law of Nations Founded on the Treaties and Customs of the Modern Nations of Europe*, English translation by William Cobbett (Philadelphia, 1795), pp. 3–5.

[2] On April 23, 1898, the United States officially informed Great Britain that it would not resort to privateering in the war with Spain and would adhere to the other "recognized rules of international law" contained in the declaration. On the same day, the Spanish Government issued a decree which, while maintaining the right to issue letters of marque, stated that the Spanish mercantile marine would be organized as auxiliary cruisers and be subject to the statutes and jurisdiction of the navy. (Moore, *International Law Digest*, Vol. 7, p. 558.)

on the customary rule of the law of nations, that treaties are binding upon the contracting parties."[1] *Pacta sunt servanda.*

Coming now to the subject-matter of treaties, not all of them can be called law-making treaties. Only such treaties may be considered as sources of international law which either stipulate new rules for future international conduct or affirm, define, or abolish existing customary or conventional rules. James Madison, in 1806, made a classification of treaties as a source of international law which has stood the test of criticism and received the highest form of approval by repetition.[2]

He says that treaties, first, may simply repeat or affirm the general law. The best known example illustrating this kind of law is the Declaration of London of March 13, 1871, which declared that "it is an essential principle of the law of nations that no Power can liberate itself from the engagements of a treaty, or modify the stipulations thereof, unless with the consent of the contracting Powers by means of an amicable arrangement."

Madison's second category consists of treaties making exceptions to the general law which, he says, constitute a particular law between the parties themselves. A striking example in recent times of treaties of this character is the series of treaties concluded by the United States with a number of nations providing, in order to aid the United States in preventing liquor smuggling, for the boarding of foreign vessels by American revenue agents beyond the three-mile limit and within an hour's sailing distance from the shore. Notwithstanding the special rights conferred by these treaties, they contain a stipulation to "uphold the principle that three marine miles extending from the coastline outwards and measured from low-water mark constitute the proper limits of territorial waters."[3]

In the third category Madison places treaties explanatory of the law of nations on points where its meaning is obscure or unsettled. Concerning such treaties, Madison says that they are, first, law between the parties themselves and, next, a sanction to the general law according to the reasonableness of the explanation and the number and character of the parties to it. There are two outstanding international documents illustrative of this category:

The first is the Declaration of Paris, already referred to. By that declaration privateering was abolished; the neutral flag was made to cover enemy goods with the exception of contraband of war, and neu-

[1] Oppenheim, *International Law* (2d ed.), Vol. I, p. 24.
[2] James Madison, *Examination of the British doctrine which subjects to capture neutral trade not open in time of peace*, Madison's *Writings*, Vol. VII, pp. 204, 236.
[3] See the convention between Great Britain and the United States of January 23, 1924. *U. S. Treaty Series*, No. 685; *Am. Jour. Int. Law*, Supp., Vol. 18 (1924), p. 127.

tral goods, with the like exception, were exempted from capture under the enemy's flag; and it was finally declared that blockades, in order to be binding, must be maintained by a force sufficient really to prevent access to the blockaded port. This declaration clarified a number of previously disputed points of maritime law. It was not accepted at the time by the United States because the United States desired to secure general recognition for the immunity of private property at sea in time of war, and it was the policy of the United States to maintain its right to commission privateers in war until the immunity of private property was generally accepted. This policy of the United States became untenable and the reasonableness of the principles contained in the Declaration of Paris eventually caused the United States to accept the declaration in full.[1]

The second example is provided by the Treaty of Washington of May 8, 1871, submitting to arbitration the claims of the United States against Great Britain for the damages inflicted during the American Civil War by cruisers of the Southern Confederacy built and equipped in British ports, these claims being generically known as the Alabama Claims. The Treaty of Washington contains three rules which were declared to be applicable to the case, as follows:

A neutral government is bound—

First, to use due diligence to prevent the fitting out, arming, or equipping, within its jurisdiction, of any vessel which it has reasonable ground to believe is intended to cruise or to carry on war against a power with which it is at peace; and also to use like diligence to prevent the departure from its jurisdiction of any vessel intended to cruise or carry on war as above, such vessel having been specially adapted, in whole or in part, within such jurisdiction, to warlike use.

Secondly, not to permit or suffer either belligerent to make use of its ports or waters as the base of naval operations against the other, or for the purpose of the renewal or augmentation of military supplies or arms, or the recruitment of men.

Thirdly, to exercise due diligence in its own ports and waters, and, as to all persons within its jurisdiction, to prevent any violation of the foregoing obligations and duties.

It is true, the Treaty of Washington declares that Great Britain "cannot assent to the foregoing rules as a statement of principles of international law which were in force at the time when the claims mentioned arose." Nevertheless the Alabama Claims arbitration tribunal awarded the sum of $15,500,000 to the United States based upon the violation of these rules, and a few years later, in 1874, the *Institut de Droit International* voted that these rules were declaratory of the law of nations.[2] These principles of international law first

---

[1] See *supra*, p. 61.

[2] For the Treaty of Washington, see Malloy, *Treaties, etc. of the United States*, Vol. I, p. 703; for the Alabama award and subsequent negotiations and discussions, see Moore, *International Law Digest*, Vol. 7, pp. 1059-76.

formally incorporated in the Treaty of Washington between Great Britain and the United States have now received formal and general recognition in the Hague Convention of 1907 concerning the Rights and Duties of Neutral Powers in Naval War.

Madison's fourth category included treaties that may be considered a voluntary or positive law of nations. In this category would be included all treaties containing general stipulations of a legally binding character, such as the conventions of the first and second Hague Peace Conferences and many like conventions which have been concluded since the World War.[1]

A fifth class of treaties not specifically included in the foregoing classification of Madison is referred to by Phillimore, who describes them as follows: "The contracting parties may introduce into a treaty expressions so generally worded as to be either explanatory of a previously contested point of law, or declaratory of the future interpretation of it, or in other ways frame the covenants of the treaty between themselves so as to lay down an universal principle binding on them, at least, in their intercourse with the rest of the world."[2]   As examples of such treaties, we may refer to the treaty of Great Britain with other powers of October 29, 1888, respecting the free navigation of the Suez Canal, and the treaty of February 5, 1900, between the United States and Great Britain for the construction of the Panama Canal, under which Great Britain as respects the Suez Canal and the United States as respects the Panama Canal stipulate that each canal is to remain free and open to vessels of all nations on terms of complete equality.

GENERAL TREATY STRUCTURE

The existing general treaty structure of the world and the particular treaties which have entered into the building of that structure can be mentioned only in a summary way.

The first law-making treaties of the modern world were concluded practically coincident with the period which marks the foundation of the modern law of nations. The Treaties of Westphalia of 1648 (the collective name for the separate treaties of Osnabrück and Münster) recognized the independence and fixed the boundaries of the separate states which had been cast adrift by the break-up of the Holy Roman Empire. Among their stipulations was one which provided that "all and each of the contracting parties to this treaty shall be held to defend and maintain all and each of the dispositions of this peace, against whomsoever it may be" (Art. 17, Treaty of Osnabrück). "Thus,"

---

[1] See *International Legislation, A Collection of the Texts of Multipartite Instruments of General Interest, beginning with the Covenant of the League of Nations*, 6 vols., edited by Manley O. Hudson and published by the Carnegie Endowment for International Peace, 1931–1937.   [2] Phillimore, *International Law* (3d ed.), Vol. I, pp. 46–9.

states Dr. David Jayne Hill, "for the first time Europe received what may be fairly described as an international constitution, which gave to all its adherents the right of intervention to enforce its arrangements." [1] It was by virtue of this article that the powers intervened during the French Revolution to prevent the spread of principles which threatened to disturb the public law of Europe founded upon the Treaties of Westphalia.

The remaking of the map of Europe following the French Revolutionary Wars took place at the Congress of Vienna in 1815. From the point of view of present international law, the Treaty of Vienna contains provisions of general interest on the following subjects:

(a) Establishment of the principle of freedom of navigation of international rivers by the commerce of all nations, subject to police regulations.

(b) A protocol dated March 19, 1815, regulating the several classes of diplomatic agents and settling their claims to precedence. This protocol was supplemented by a subsequent protocol of the Congress of Aix-la-Chapelle, dated November 21, 1818.

(c) A declaration on the universal abolition of the slave trade.

The doctrine of intervention sanctioned by the Treaty of Osnabrück and applied during the French Revolution met with the determined opposition of the first non-European government to be admitted to the family of nations. When the doctrine was formally revived in the Holy Alliance of 1815 and the parties to that alliance threatened to extend the principle to the revolted Spanish colonies in America, President Monroe, in his famous message of December 2, 1823, declared the policy of the United States with regard to Europe to be "not to interfere in the internal concerns of any of its powers," and that the United States would consider any attempt on the part of those powers to extend their system to any portion of the Western Hemisphere as dangerous to the peace and safety of the United States. Consequently, as pointed out by Moore, "much that is found on the subject of intervention in the books on international law is specially applicable to the situation in Europe, and can be applied only indirectly or by analogy to the situation in America or in other parts of the non-European world." [2] Whatever may be the objections of the Latin American nations to the varying interpretations that have been placed upon the Monroe Doctrine from time to time, the nations of the Western Hemisphere are opposed in principle to the doctrine of intervention, against which the Monroe Doctrine was originally aimed. On December 26, 1933, the Seventh International Conference of

[1] David Jayne Hill, *History of European Diplomacy*, Vol. 2 (1906), p. 602.
[2] Moore, *International Law Digest*, Vol. 6, p. 2.

American States, adopted at Montevideo a convention on the rights and duties of states, which declares that "no state has the right to intervene in the internal and external affairs of another." [1] This declaration was reaffirmed at the Inter-American Conference for the Maintenance of Peace, held at Buenos Aires in December, 1936. [2]

The navigation of international rivers, the freedom of which was proclaimed by the Congress of Vienna of 1815, is a subject which typifies very well the development of conventional international law. The principle of free navigation was then applied to the Rhine, and later extended to the Danube by the Treaty of Paris of 1856. Various treaties between the United States and Great Britain have been concluded in regard to the navigation of the rivers of North America, and the nations of South America have likewise entered into important treaty stipulations in regard to the great rivers of that continent. Reviewing the practice of maritime states during the century or more preceding the World War of 1914–1918, Dr. Charles Cheney Hyde concludes: (1) that any right of navigation is dependent upon the consent of the territorial sovereign; (2) that the law of nations imposes upon such sovereign the duty to consent to the navigation of its own waters by the inhabitants of any upstream riparian state; (3) that where a river and its tributaries afford the sole means of water communication between several riparian states and the ocean, it becomes the duty of any lower riparian state to consent to free access to countries upstream by foreign merchant vessels; and (4) that in the absence of international regulation, the territorial sovereign may control navigation within its own waters. [3]

The treaties of peace which ended the World War included general and detailed provisions to assure freedom of navigation of international rivers. The treaties specified certain rivers which were declared to be international, and on the waterways thus declared to be international, the treaties stipulated that "the nationals, property and flags of all powers shall be treated on a footing of perfect equality, no distinction being made to the detriment of the nationals, property or flag of any power between them and the nationals, property or flag of the riparian state itself or of the most favored nation." [4] The régime set up in the Treaty of Versailles was superseded by the convention and statute on the régime of navigable waters of international concern signed at Barce-

[1] Seventh International Conference of American States, Montevideo, Uruguay, December 3–26, 1933, *Final Act, including the Conventions and Additional Protocol adopted by the Conference*, p. 187.
[2] See Additional Protocol relative to Non-Intervention, signed December 23, 1936. Pan American Union, *Congress and Conference Series*, No. 22, p. 34.
[3] *Am. Jour. Int. Law*, Vol. 4 (1910), pp. 154–5.
[4] Art. 332 of the Treaty of Versailles, June 28, 1919. Like provisions will be found in the other peace treaties.

lona on April 20, 1921, pursuant to the provisions of Article 338 of the Treaty of Versailles. The Barcelona Convention came into force on October 31, 1922. The annexed statute contains twenty-five articles of detailed regulations which may be regarded as the codification of international law on this subject for the nations which have signed and ratified the convention.[1]

Intimately associated with the freedom of navigation is the right of commercial intercourse; in fact most bilateral treaties granting the right of navigation also contain provisions concerning the commercial relations between the contracting countries, and such treaties are usually called treaties of commerce and navigation. It is believed that this class of treaties constitutes the largest group in the calendar of treaty subjects. Some idea of the extent of treaty-making in this field may be obtained by examining the collection of treaties of commerce and navigation concluded by Great Britain with foreign powers, the compilation of which was started by Lewis Hertslet, librarian of the British Foreign Office. The first volume was published in 1827; and the earliest treaty in the collection is the Treaty of Peace and Commerce between Great Britain and Portugal of 1642. The series was continued under the title of Hertslet's *Commercial Treaties* until 1925 (Volume 31), after which it was incorporated with the *British and Foreign State Papers*. Treaties of commerce and navigation contain provisions on a variety of subjects, such as the use of ports, the rights of aliens to travel, reside, and carry on business, customs tariffs, taxes and other charges, consular officers, fisheries, etc.

In recent years, treaty-making has become more specialized and there has grown up a great body of treaties dealing with topics which were formerly included in conventions of commerce and navigation. To be especially noted as a large and important class are consular treaties, which often also include stipulations concerning the rights of aliens. The growth of the consular system is a good index of the phenomenal extension of travel, residence, and business abroad made necessary by the demands of modern commerce. In the year 1931 there were 17,442 consular officers sent by sixty states and distributed among 850 cities and towns.[2]

A glance at the treaty series published by the individual governments, of which there are now a number, will show the innumerable subjects upon which separate pairs or groups of states now have binding treaty stipulations. The subjects are as various in their nature as

[1] For the text of the Barcelona Convention and Statute, see League of Nations Document, C.479.M.327.1921. VIII.; *Am. Jour. Int. Law*, Supp., Vol. 18 (1924), p. 151; Hudson, *International Legislation* (1931), Vol. I, p. 638.

[2] Legal Position and Functions of Consuls, Harvard Research in International Law, published in *Am. Jour. Int. Law*, Supp., Vol. 26 (1932), p. 201.

are the relations which exist between neighboring countries and their peoples. They cover practically every means of interstate communication and intercourse.

International relations of more world-wide interest and concern are the subject of general agreements concluded by larger groups of states. There is scarcely any phase of international life which is not now touched by a general treaty or convention. Considering for the present treaties of a non-political character, some of the more important treaties regulating the peaceful relations of nations will be enumerated. The time of day is regulated by a protocol signed at Washington in October, 1884, which fixed the prime meridian. In addition to the numerous bilateral commercial treaties already referred to, there are general treaties dealing with such subjects as maritime ports, import and export prohibitions and restrictions, customs formalities, false indications of origins of goods, and the regulation of weights and measures. All forms of international communications are the subject of regulations prescribed by general conventions which deal with postal facilities (now extended to include parcels post and money orders), cables, telegraphs and telephones, radiotelegraphy, international railways, the circulation of motor vehicles, and aërial navigation. Industry which crosses state boundaries is brought under control by general conventions such as those regulating night work for women, the use of poisonous substances in manufactures, the development of hydraulic power, the transmission of electrical power, workman's compensation insurance, and an International Labor Organization has been established to seek to better the conditions of the laboring classes in the respective countries as a necessary condition of promoting harmony between nations. Patents and trade-marks, literary and artistic property are protected by a number of general conventions. International coöperation in the suppression of crime is provided, in addition to many bilateral extradition treaties, by general conventions such as those dealing with the traffic in women and children and for the suppression of counterfeiting. Public health is safeguarded by international conventions prescribing sanitary measures for the protection not only of human beings but of animals and plants, as well as by those relating to pharmacopœial and chemical formulas. The scope of general treaties extends even to the protection of morals in such conventions as those for the suppression of the traffic in opium and other narcotic drugs and of the circulation of obscene publications.

The conduct of private affairs extending beyond state boundary lines is aided by general conventions on such subjects as judicial assistance, civil procedure, and commercial arbitration. Conflicts of law in different countries in such matters as marriage and divorce, guardianship of minors, bills of exchange and checks, are reduced or eliminated by a series of general conventions on private international law.

The law of the sea in time of peace has evolved into a separate branch of the law now generally referred to as maritime law. There are general conventions prescribing the rules of the road at sea, maritime signals, and regulations for the safety of life at sea. Other general conventions deal with the treatment of merchant seamen, the loading of vessels, maintenance of lighthouses, bills of lading, maritime mortgages and liens, collisions at sea, and the liability of shipowners.

A similar development has taken place with respect to the laws of war. The original Red Cross Convention of 1864 for the amelioration of the condition of the sick and wounded of armies in the field has passed through several revisions, the last being that of Geneva, signed on July 27, 1929. The principles of the Geneva Red Cross Conventions were adapted to maritime warfare by the Hague Conventions of 1899 and 1907. At Geneva in 1929, a separate convention was drawn up and signed on July 27 relating to the treatment of prisoners of war.

Starting with the *Instructions for the Government of the Armies of the United States in the Field*, issued as General Orders No. 100 by the United States War Department during the American Civil War, there have been several codifications of the laws of war on land. An official conference at Brussels in 1874 formulated a code based upon the American instructions, which later became incorporated in the Hague Conventions of 1899 and 1907 respecting the laws and customs of war on land. The Hague Conference of 1907 also adopted a convention respecting the rights and duties of neutral powers and persons in case of war on land.

The Declaration of Paris of 1856, already referred to, contained statements of rules of naval warfare as between neutrals and belligerents which have since been universally accepted as principles of international law. Additional codifications of the laws of war at sea are contained in the Hague Conventions of 1907 relating to the status of enemy merchant ships on the outbreak of hostilities, the conversion of merchant ships into warships, the laying of submarine mines, bombardment by naval forces, and certain restrictions on the right of capture. The Hague Conference of 1907 also adopted a convention concerning the rights and duties of neutral powers in naval war. A formidable attempt was made at the London Naval Conference of 1908–1909 to state in conventional form the generally recognized principles of international law applicable in naval warfare as a prerequisite to the establishment of the international court of prize provided for in the Hague Convention of 1907. Notwithstanding the failure of the ratification of the Declaration of London, signed on

February 26, 1909, the provisions of the declaration restated in many instances the rules of customary international law which are binding irrespective of the non-ratification of the declaration. The same situation is true of the Hague Conventions of 1899 and 1907 which, for some technical reason, may not be binding upon a particular belligerent.

Although there were repeated charges and counter-charges of violations of the laws of war during the World War, the Peace Conference of Paris of 1919 made no attempt to deal with the laws of war, and the peace treaties were drafted upon the assumption that the establishment of the League of Nations would relegate to a position of relative unimportance the laws of war and neutrality. Those treaties therefore contain no provision on these subjects.

But the continuation of the effort to control the methods of warfare was renewed at the Conference on the Limitation of Armaments held in Washington, November 12, 1921, to February 6, 1922. On the latter date, France, Great Britain, Italy, Japan, and the United States signed a treaty to prohibit the use of submarines and of poisonous gases in future wars. At the same time, the five powers adopted a resolution to constitute a commission of jurists to consider the amendment of the laws of war so as to cover new methods of attack or defense. This commission met at The Hague on December 11, 1922, and considered the subjects of aviation and radio in war. The commission adjourned on February 19, 1923, after adopting one set of rules for the control of radio in time of war, and another set of rules on aërial warfare. Neither the treaty signed in Washington in 1922 nor the Hague rules of 1923 have gone into force because of lack of ratification. The treaty for the limitation and reduction of naval armament, signed at London on April 22, 1930, by the United States, Great Britain, Japan, France, and Italy, and ratified by the three first named powers, establishes rules of international law to govern the use of submarines in war.[1]

Separate and distinct efforts have been made in the Western Hemisphere to conventionalize the relations of the American Republics both in war and peace. The movement began as early as 1826 with the Congress of Panama, which was followed by a number of international conferences held on various subjects and attended by representatives of

[1] *U. S. Treaty Series*, No. 830; *Am. Jour. Int. Law*, Supp., Vol. 25 (1931), p. 78. The treaty of London of April 22, 1930, remained in force until December 31, 1936, when it ceased to be effective because of non-renewal. However, Part IV, which established the rules of international law to govern submarines in war, remains in force "without limit of time." (Art. 23.) On November 6, 1936, representatives of the signatories of the treaty of April 22, 1930, namely, the United States, Great Britain and the British Dominions, France, Italy, and Japan, met in London and signed a protocol requesting the British Government to communicate the rules to all governments which are not signatories of the treaty and invite them to accede thereto. (*New York Times*, November 7, 1936, p. 6; *British Parliamentary Papers*, Cmd. 5302.)

varying numbers of states.[1]   In 1889 there was inaugurated the series
of Pan American Conferences officially called the International Conferences of American States.   Starting at Washington in that year, these
conferences have been held at irregular intervals in different American
capitals, the seventh having taken place at Montevideo, Uruguay, in
December, 1933.   General conventions on many subjects of both
private and public international law have been adopted at these
conferences.[2]   An extraordinary Inter-American Conference for the
Maintenance of Peace was held in Buenos Aires in December, 1936.[3]

It would be a stupendous task to undertake to examine all treaties
and attempt to prepare a statement of principles of international law
which they evidence in the practice of states.   A glance at any of the
general collections of published treaties will give some idea of the
tremendous amount and variety of treaty material now in existence.[4]
Dumont's *Corps universel diplomatique du droit des gens*, with supplements by Rousset, Wenck's *Codex Juris Gentium*, and the several collections and series bearing the name of De Martens (*Recueil, Recueil
général*, and *Nouveau recueil général*), supply in continuous succession
the texts of the more important treaties from the reign of Charlemagne
to the present time.   A chronological list of the contents of these collections published by M. Tétot in 1866–73[5] discloses that at that date
they contained 7,421 treaties.   Figures are not available as to the
number of treaties appearing in these collections from 1866 to the
present time, but in view of the greatly accelerated pace in the conclusion of treaties during the twentieth century, the total number of
treaty texts of this character must now exceed ten thousand.   The
Treaty Series of the League of Nations, which includes treaties registered with the Secretariat pursuant to Article 18 of the Covenant,
numbered 3,824 at the end of the year 1936, indicating presumably that
treaties to that number at least are in force throughout the world.

It was this growing body of treaty material, coupled with the recommendation of the Committee of Jurists which drafted the Statute of
the Permanent Court of International Justice in 1920, that a new series
of conferences for the advancement of international law be held in suc-

[1] A summary of these Latin American conferences is given in "The Codification
of International Law in the Americas," by Raul D'Eca, in the magazine *World Affairs*,
June, 1935, p. 94; also in *Special Handbook for the Use of Delegates, Inter-American
Conference for the Maintenance of Peace, Buenos Aires, December 1, 1936*, prepared by
the Pan American Union, Washington, D. C.

[2] For a tabulation of the work of the first six Pan American Conferences, see *International Conferences of the American States, 1889–1928*, published by the Carnegie
Endowment for International Peace in 1931.   For the work of the Seventh Conference, see Seventh International Conference of American States, *Final Act, etc., supra.*

[3] See Pan American Union, *Congress and Conference Series*, No. 22.

[4] See *Manual of Collections of Treaties and of Collections relating to Treaties*, compiled
by Denys P. Myers (1922).   [5] *Répertoire des traités* (1866–73).

cession to the Hague Conferences of 1899 and 1907, which induced the Assembly of the League of Nations on September 22, 1924, to propose the codification of international law, which in turn resulted in the subsequent appointment of the League of Nations Committee for the Progressive Codification of International Law.

As the result of the work of that committee of the League of Nations, an official conference for the codification of international law was held at The Hague from March 13 to April 13, 1930. The following three subjects selected by the committee were placed upon the agenda of the conference: nationality, territorial waters, and responsibility of states for damages caused in their territory to the person or property of foreigners. The conference failed to achieve any immediate results in the process of officially codifying international law and no further conferences for this purpose have been arranged by the League of Nations.[1]

But the movement for codification of international law was kept alive elsewhere. In 1926 the American Institute of International Law drafted thirty projects of conventions on as many subjects, which were laid before the official Commission of American Jurists at Rio de Janeiro in 1927. From this commission emanated twelve projects which in turn were submitted to the Sixth International Conference of American States meeting at Habana in 1928, and that conference adopted seven conventions on the following subjects: status of aliens, duties and rights of states in the event of civil strife, treaties, diplomatic officers, consular agents, maritime neutrality, and asylum. At the Seventh Pan American Conference, held in Montevideo in 1933, additional conventions were adopted dealing with the rights and duties of states, nationality, extradition, and political asylum. Moreover, a resolution was adopted at that conference officially providing methods for the future codification of international law by the American Republics coöperating through the Pan American Union.

Before passing from the attempts at codification of international law, further mention should be made of some of the outstanding private efforts to this end.

The *Institut de Droit International* was organized in Ghent in 1873 for the express purpose of giving aid to the growth of international law and assisting in its progressive codification. The Institute, composed of distinguished members of the profession from many countries, has held forty meetings in various countries, at which, after careful consideration and discussion, resolutions and projects have been adopted on a great many topics of international law. Some of these carefully pre-

---

[1] For the results of the Codification Conference, see the series of articles by the American delegates and advisers which appeared in the *Am. Jour. Int. Law*, Vol. 24 (1930), pp. 447, 467, 486, 500, 674.

pared projects have been the bases of the work of official international conferences, especially those held at The Hague in 1899 and 1907.[1]

Another body was organized in 1873 at Brussels under the title Association for the Reform and Codification of the Law of Nations. The main object of this association was to provide a code of international law as a preliminary step in the substitution of international arbitration for war. It later gave considerable attention to subjects of private international law and has to its credit commendable achievements in the unification of the rules of general average and on bills of exchange. Its name was later changed to the International Law Association, and after the World War it directed its efforts toward the codification of public international law. It has held thirty-eight conferences and the printed proceedings of these meetings contain the texts of a number of projects for the codification of important topics of international law.[2]

Mention should also be made of the Harvard Research in International Law, organized under the auspices of the faculty of the Harvard Law School. This organization was started in 1927 and 1928 for the purpose of preparing the draft of an international convention on each of the subjects which had been placed on the agenda for the codification of international law at The Hague in 1930. The Research has the assistance of an Advisory Committee of about fifty of the leading members of the bar and faculties of other American colleges and universities, which passes upon the final results. The draft conventions with comments are published in Supplements to the *American Journal of International Law*. In 1929 the Research covered in this way the subjects of nationality, responsibility of states for injuries to foreigners, and territorial waters. In 1932 draft conventions with comments were published on diplomatic privileges and immunities, legal position and functions of consuls, competence of courts in regard to foreign states, and piracy. In 1935 draft conventions with comments were published

---

[1] See the *Annuaires* of the Institute, and *Resolutions of the Institute of International Law* collected and published by the Carnegie Endowment for International Peace in 1916.

[2] The following are the annuals of the chief international law associations:

Annuaire de l'Institut de Droit International, Brussels (39 vols., 1875–1936); *International Law Association, Reports of Conferences*, London (1873–1934); *Proceedings of the American Society of International Law*, Washington (29 vols., 1908–1936); *Grotius Annuaire international*, The Hague (22 vols., 1913–1936); *The Grotius Society, Transactions*, London (21 vols., 1916–1936); *L'Union Juridique Internationale, Séances et Travaux*, Paris, 1920–1935; *British Year Book of International Law*, London (issued under the auspices of the Royal Institute of International Affairs, 17 vols., 1920–1936); *American Branch of the International Law Association, Reports of Proceedings*, New York, 1922–1935 (proceedings of other branches of the Association are published in various countries); *Académie Diplomatique Internationale, Séances et Travaux*, Paris, 1927–1935; *Annuaire de l'Association Yougoslave de Droit International*, Belgrade-Paris (2 vols., 1931–1934); *Proceedings of the Australian and New Zealand Society of International Law*, Melbourne, Vol. I, 1935.

on the subjects of extradition, jurisdiction with respect to crime, and the law of treaties. The comments which accompany each of these subjects include an historical introduction, critical and analytical discussions of each article proposed with annotations to important authorities, and a comprehensive bibliography of the available literature in the principal languages.

The resolution of the Assembly of the League of Nations adopted September 22, 1924, referred to the "legislative needs of international relations," and another resolution adopted later by the Ninth Assembly on September 24, 1928, expressed the great immediate practical value, in connection with the codification of international law, of assembling together the various general international conventions in the form of a code. But the Assembly quickly changed its mind as to the feasibility of such a project, and a year later adopted a resolution which concluded that such publication could not at present be achieved in a satisfactory manner.

A century ago, Henry Wheaton thought it impossible that there could be a code of international law, one of his reasons being that the nations had not organized any paramount legislative authority for the purpose of expressly declaring international law. By 1907, however, John Bassett Moore stated one of the modes by which international law may be developed to be "the specific adoption of a rule of action by an act in its nature legislative" and, he added, that "the past century has been specially distinguished by the modification and improvement of international law by what may be called acts of international legislation."[1]

The term "international legislation" has more recently been applied to all multipartite international instruments of general interest resulting from the work of international conferences. The nature of such acts and the change in conditions of modern international life from which they have evolved as sources of international law are explained as follows by Judge Manley O. Hudson, who has been a pioneer in collecting and editing such instruments:

The conception of a law of nations consciously constructed by a community of states found little place in the writings of the seventeenth and eighteenth centuries, and it has been but slowly evolved out of the experience of the nineteenth century. The needs of the international society of earlier times had not been thought to call for effort to develop new law; but the revolutionary changes of the nineteenth century created a new international society, with which came the need for a different kind of international law. Such changes are still in progress; the industrial revolution of the nineteenth century is being paralleled, in its effect on international relations, by the technical revolution of the twentieth century; and as new conditions are produced, or old conditions are changed, need arises for new law. The customary guidance does not fully serve this need; nor are courts able to fill it. Law-making, legislation, has come to be a process quite as impor-

[1] *Am. Jour. Int. Law*, Vol. 1 (1907), pp. 11–12.

tant in the development of the law of nations as administration, or arbitration, or adjudication. Whether expressly or otherwise, no study of international law in the twentieth century can ignore legislation as one of its principal sources.[1]

For the half of a century which preceded the World War, Judge Hudson lists 257 international instruments of this character, while for the ten years following the Covenant of the League of Nations he reproduces 229 instruments of similar character. Judge Hudson does not claim that there is yet in existence a single international legislature comparable in its authority to a national legislature; but concerning the agencies of international legislation, he says that "two or more states may lay down a law for themselves by the use of any agency available for that purpose, or of an agency created *ad hoc*. They may employ the usual diplomatic channels for the consultation which is necessary; they may conduct this consultation in an international conference specially organized for the purpose; they may agree upon the provisions of new law at a meeting of such a body as the Assembly of the League of Nations." And, reasoning by analogy, he maintains that "it is certainly not necessary that a legislative agency be permanent; nor that it be endowed with general powers; nor that it proceed in any particular manner; nor that it have authority over states not represented; nor that the result of its efforts, when agreement is reached, become immediately executory." Those who believe that international law has and will develop along lines analogous to the growth of municipal law must substantially agree with Judge Hudson's conclusion that "historically the customary elements of both national and international law have given way to legislation." [2]

On the question of the sanctions of international legislation, Judge Hudson takes the same view as that expressed by the Chief Justice of Hongkong in the case of the *Prometheus, supra,* with regard to the sanction of customary international law. As to the contention that legislation can exist only when it is supported by some power to enforce it, Judge Hudson says that "no such test can be applied to national legislation," and he argues that "it would seem to be no more applicable to international legislation." "When the will of two or more states is properly declared," he continues, "the declaration seems to be binding on the states concerned, in their relations to which it applies, because of a general principle of international law that states must keep faith with each other. The juristic force of the declaration is not lost because one of the states concerned may fail to observe it, no more than national legislation would lose its force because of a violation." He concludes that "an intention to observe its international obligations would seem to be . . . a condition of membership in the society of nations." [3]

[1] *International Legislation* (1931), Vol. I, p. xiii.
[2] *Ibid.*, pp. xiv–xv.   [3] *Ibid.*, p. xvii.

CHAPTER VI

INTERNATIONAL LAW IN THE COURTS

As a source of international law, the decisions of courts represent, for the most part, a phenomenon of the rapid growth of the science in comparatively recent years. It was only ninety years ago when Henry Wheaton wrote that "as nations acknowledge no superior, as they have not organized any common paramount authority, for the purpose of establishing by an express declaration their international law, and as they have not constituted any sort of Amphictyonic magistracy to interpret and apply that law, it is impossible that there should be a code of international law illustrated by judicial interpretations."[1] Wheaton's only reference to court decisions as a source of international law was to "the adjudications of international tribunals, such as boards of arbitration and courts of prize." Concerning these two sources, he said that "greater weight is justly attributable to the judgments of mixed tribunals, appointed by the joint consent of two nations . . . than to those of admiralty courts established by and dependent on the instructions of one nation only."[2] This statement of an author who, thirty years before, had written and published *A Digest of the Law of Maritime Captures and Prizes*, in which he asserted that "the law of prize is the most important practical branch of the law of nations,"[3] reflects the undeveloped state of international law at that period.

Following the historical order, the decisions of prize courts will be referred to as sources of international law before the decisions of other national courts are discussed.

PRIZE COURTS

As in the case of war on land, war at sea was formerly not conducted wholly by governmental instrumentalities, that is, by ships publicly built and maintained for that purpose. It was the common practice of belligerents to commission private vessels for the purpose of harassing and capturing the commerce of the enemy. Crude rules for this often profitable form of mercenary warfare were developed in the early sea codes and may be found in the *Consolato del Mare*. With the spread of commerce at sea between nations, the belligerent's right to seize the property of his enemy was extended to interference in the trade of neutrals which might be of assistance to the enemy in the war. It was not until the Declaration of Paris in 1856, however, that a general international agreement was reached in regard to neutral and belligerent

[1] Wheaton, *Elements of International Law* (3d ed., 1846), p. 3.   [2] *Ibid.*, p. 26.
[3] New York, M'Dermut & Arden (1815), p. iii.

rights at sea, and that agreement marked the development of navies to
the point of efficiency where governments were ready to abolish privateering.

Prize courts had been established and functioned under rules of
procedure from the middle of the sixteenth century,[1] but their decisions did not assume importance as sources of international law until
the publication of Lord Stowell's famous judgments was begun at the
end of the eighteenth century.

In the leading case of *The Maria*, also known as the Swedish Convoy,
Lord Stowell, in 1799, judicially stated the character of the court over
which he presided, and the nature of the law he was called upon to administer. He said:

I trust that it has not escaped my anxious recollection for one moment what
it is that the duty of my station calls for from me—namely, to consider myself as
stationed here, not to deliver occasional and shifting opinions to serve present
purposes of particular national interest, but to administer with indifference that
justice which the law of nations holds out, without distinction to independent
states, some happening to be neutral and some to be belligerent. The seat of
judicial authority is, indeed, locally here, in the belligerent country, according to
the known law and practice of nations; but the law itself has no locality. It is
the duty of the person who sits here to determine this question exactly as he
would determine the same question if sitting at Stockholm; to assert no pretensions on the part of Great Britain which he would not allow to Sweden in the
same circumstances, and to impose no duties on Sweden, as a neutral country,
which he would not admit to belong to Great Britain in the same character.[2]

The reasons for this dual character of prize courts appear when we
consider the nature of the jurisdiction which they exercise. The acts
of a belligerent power in the right of war are not justiciable in its own
courts unless such power submit to their jurisdiction; the acts done
under the authority of one sovereign are not subject to revision by
the tribunals of another sovereign; and the parties to such acts are
not responsible therefor in their private capacities. "It follows that
but for the existence of Courts of Prize no one aggrieved by the acts
of a belligerent power in times of war could obtain redress otherwise
than through diplomatic channels and at the risk of disturbing international amity. An appropriate remedy is, however, provided by the
fact that, according to international law, every belligerent power must
appoint and submit to the jurisdiction of a prize court to which any
person aggrieved by its acts has access."[3] This duty of the prize court
to administer international and not municipal law came before the

[1] See "The Early Development of the Law of Neutral Rights," by P. C. Jessup and
Francis Deák, *Political Science Quarterly*, December, 1931.

[2] High Court of Admiralty, 1 C. Rob. 340; Dickinson, *Cases on the Law of Nations*
(1929), p. 39; Fenwick, *Cases on International Law* (1935), p. 791; Scott, *Cases on International Law* (1922), p. 1003.

[3] Justice Story in the case of *The Invincible*, 44 Fed. Cas. No. 7,054.

British Prize Court during the World War, and was reaffirmed by the Privy Council in the case of *The Zamora*.[1]

The American courts take the same attitude. In a prize case which arose during the Spanish American War, on appeal to the Supreme Court of the United States that court held: "International law is part of our law, and must be ascertained and administered by the courts of justice of appropriate jurisdiction, as often as questions of right depending upon it are duly presented for their determination." [2]

France has always played a leading rôle in the development of prize law; but in civil law countries the prize courts are not as completely judicial as those of the common law countries, and may be partly administrative in character.[3] For this reason the ordinances of these nations are of great importance to show the law as understood and applied by them. The most famous ordinance of this character was that of Louis XIV issued in 1681. It was compiled from the ancient French marine ordinances beginning in 1400, and thus connected the maritime institutions of the seventeenth century with the ancient laws and customs of the sea compiled in the fourteenth century by the authors of the *Consolato del Mare*. It contains a complete collection of the rules and principles of prize law which had been gradually formed by ancient usages and judicial precedents. While it was intended only for the guidance of the French courts, its influence spread to other countries, and Wheaton called it a "beautiful model" of marine legislation. Its contents were enriched by the *Commentaire* of Valin, published in 1760. This French author has been freely drawn upon by the writers of other countries, especially of England and the United States, and the ordinance itself is often cited by the courts as an important source document.[4] A few years previously a work of the same character had been published in Cadiz dealing with the Spanish conception of the law of prize.[5] In 1763, Valin published a collection of French prize ordinances from the earliest times down to that period in his *Traité des prises*. A new edition of his *Commentaire* was published in 1766, the year after his death. Another edition of the *Traité des prises* was edited in 1855 by Pistoye and Duverdy, which was revised in 1859 following the Declaration of Paris.[6]

---

[1] 2 Appeal Cases, 1916, p. 77.

[2] *The Paquete Habana* (1900), 175 U. S. 677; Dickinson, *Cases on the Law of Nations* (1929), p. 42; Fenwick, *Cases on International Law* (1935), p. 12; Scott, *Cases on International Law* (1922), p. 12.

[3] For the organization and jurisdiction of prize courts in various countries, and a discussion of the law they administer, see *Treatise on the Law of Prize*, by C. J. Colombos (1926).

[4] *Commentaire sur l'Ordonnance de la marine du mois d'août 1681.*

[5] Felix Joseph de Abreu, *Tratado jurídico-político sobre pressas de mar.*

[6] The French ordinances and regulations, and the decisions of the French prize courts, are published in continuous collections of the *arrêts* of the *Conseil d'Etat* and the *Conseil des Prises*.

The interpretation and application of prize law by the courts of different countries inevitably leads to divergencies of opinion and practice. An effort was consequently made at the Hague Peace Conference of 1907 to establish an International Court of Prize with appellate jurisdiction over the decisions of national prize courts which might be appealed from by neutral governments and private individuals of both neutral and enemy character. The convention provided that the International Prize Court (Article 7) should apply treaties and international law, or, in the absence of these two sources of the law, the general principles of justice and equity. This definition of the law was not acceptable to the British Government, and the London Naval Conference was called in 1908 for the purpose of agreeing upon the law to be applied by the international court. The Declaration of London was signed on February 26, 1909, but Great Britain refused to ratify it, and it never became effective.[1]

During the World War some fifteen hundred decisions were rendered by the prize courts of the belligerent nations. The texts have been collected and published, and several treatises deal especially with them.[2]

Whether the Permanent Court of International Justice now established at The Hague will have jurisdiction of appeals from national prize courts in future war remains to be determined. This question was discussed in a memorandum which accompanied the signature of the British Government to the Optional Clause of the Statute of the court. In that memorandum the British Government took the position that the laws of neutrality had been so changed by the Covenant of the League of Nations and the Pact of Paris for the Renunciation of War that there seemed no ground for the apprehension that the operations of the British Navy in time of war would be hampered "by exposing the legitimacy of British belligerent action at sea to the decision of an international court."[3] The United States Government promptly made public a statement denying that the argument in the British memorandum concerning changes in the laws of neutrality applied to the position of the United States as a signatory of the Pact of Paris.[4] Of course, as long as the United States does not adhere to

[1] For text of the Declaration of London see *British Parl. Papers*, Misc. No. 4 (1909), Cmd. 4554; *Am. Jour. Int. Law*, Supp., Vol. 3 (1909), p. 179. The United States Senate advised and consented to the ratification of the International Prize Court Convention on February 15, 1911, and of the Declaration of London on April 24, 1912, both without reservation.

[2] See *Jurisprudence en matière de prises maritimes*, containing in French translation the decisions rendered during the World War by the prize courts of France, Great Britain, Italy, and Germany, collected by M. Paul Fauchille, and published in Paris beginning in 1916. For digests and discussions of the cases decided during the World War, see *Le droit des prises de la Grande Guerre* (1924), by J. H. W. Verzijl, and *Prize Law during the World War* (1927), by James W. Garner.

[3] Misc. No. 12 (1929), Cmd. 3452; *Am. Jour. Int. Law*, Supp., Vol. 25 (1931), p. 82.

[4] The text of Secretary of State Stimson's statement of December 30, 1929, is reprinted in the Supplement to the *Am. Jour. Int. Law*, Vol. 25 (1931), p. 90, note.

the Statute of the Permanent Court and its Optional Clause, the court can have no jurisdiction of prize cases to which the United States or its citizens may be a party.

NATIONAL COURTS

The decisions of national courts in times of peace and war have come to be included among the sources of international law even more recently than the decisions of prize courts in time of war. The reason for this is not difficult to find, for it is inherent in the definition of international law which generally prevails, although not universally accepted, which excludes individuals as subjects of international law. This is stated very definitely by Oppenheim, who says "since the law of nations is based on the common consent of individual states, and not of individual human beings, states solely and exclusively are the subjects of international law. This means that the law of nations is a law for the international conduct of states, and not of their citizens." [1] A similar statement was made by Wheaton, but a European contemporary of Wheaton took issue with that view. August Wilhelm Heffter, professor of law at the Universities of Bonn and Berlin, divided international law into two branches, in which he gave precedence to "human rights in general, and those private relations which sovereign states recognize in respect to individuals not subject to their authority." It is interesting to note, in passing, that Heffter rejected the term "international law" and based his system upon the *jus gentium* of Roman jurisprudence. "This law," he says, "is applied not merely to regulate the mutual relations of states, but also of individuals, so far as concerns their respective rights and duties." [2]

There are limitations of jurisdiction inhering in the character of national courts as one branch only of the national government which as a complete entity is the subject of international law. These limitations should be understood at the outset.

It is a principle of national law that the sovereign is not amenable in his own courts, except with his consent. This principle extends beyond national boundaries, and we have the principle of international law that a sovereign cannot be sued in the courts of a foreign state. This principle was conveniently summarized by the English Court of Appeals in 1880, when it held:

As a consequence of the absolute independence of every sovereign authority and of the international comity which induces every sovereign state to respect the independence of every other sovereign state, each state declines to exercise by means of any of its courts any of its territorial jurisdiction over the person

---

[1] International Law (2d ed.), Vol. I, p. 19.
[2] Heffter, *Das europäische Völkerrecht*, cited in Wheaton, *Elements of International Law* (Dana ed., 1866), p. 16.

of any sovereign or ambassador, or over the public property of any state which is destined to its public use, or over the property of any ambassador, though such sovereign, ambassador, or property be within its territory.[1]

The same principle had been stated at length by the Supreme Court of the United States in 1812 in the case of the Schooner Exchange v. M'Faddon.[2] It had also been applied by the *Cour de Cassation* of France in 1849 in the case of the Gouvernement Espagnol v. Lambège et Pujol,[3] and it was invoked by the German *Kompetenzgerichtshof* in the case of Von Hellfeld v. Russland (*The Anhalt* case), decided in 1910.[4]

The sovereign, of course, appears in his own courts as prosecutor of the private individual in criminal cases, and often brings civil actions against him. Likewise, a foreign sovereign may sue an individual in the court of another nation, and in either case the individual is entitled to make his proper defenses; but national courts are not open to suits by one sovereign against another, except by mutual consent.

The Constitution of the United States (Art. III, Sec. 2) expressly confers jurisdiction upon the Supreme Court in suits between a state of the American Union and foreign states; yet that court has recently held that a foreign state cannot bring a suit against a state of the American Union without the consent of both the American state and the Federal Government. The court ruled that—

The National Government, by virtue of its control of our foreign relations is entitled to employ the resources of diplomatic negotiations and to effect such an international settlement as may be found to be appropriate, through treaty, agreement of arbitration, or otherwise. It cannot be supposed that it was the intention that a controversy growing out of the action of a State, which involves a matter of national concern and which is said to affect injuriously the interests of a foreign state, or a dispute arising from conflicting claims of a State of the Union and a foreign state as to territorial boundaries, should be taken out of the sphere of international negotiations and adjustment through a resort by the foreign state to a suit under the provisions of Section 2 of Article III. In such a case, the State has immunity from suit without her consent and the National Government is protected by the provision prohibiting agreements between States and Foreign Powers in the absence of the consent of the Congress.[5]

It is not unknown for two nations to refer a dispute between them to the decision of a municipal court of one of them. A case which arose between Holland and the United States out of the World War was referred by agreement to the Court of Claims of the United States. In October, 1917, the United States authorities at the port of New

---

[1] *The Parlement Belge*, L. R. 5 Prob. Div. (1880); Fenwick, *Cases on International Law* (1935), p. 333; Scott, *Cases on International Law* (1922), p. 310, note.
[2] 7 Cranch 116. [3] Dalloz, *Jurisprudence générale*, 1849, I. 5.
[4] *Am. Jour. Int. Law*, Vol. 5 (1911), p. 490.
[5] Principality of Monaco v. The State of Mississippi (1934), 292 U. S. 313; *Am. Jour. Int. Law*, Vol. 28 (1934), p. 576.

York refused to grant clearance to a vessel of the Royal Holland Lloyd and detained the vessel at that port.   The Dutch Government claimed damages from the United States Government, which finally requisitioned the vessel in March, 1918.[1]   By agreement of the two governments, and pursuant to a special Act of Congress approved March 3, 1927, jurisdiction was conferred upon the United States Court of Claims "to hear and determine such suit to judgment."   The Court of Claims rendered its judgment on December 7, 1931.   Although the United States Government was not liable to the Royal Holland Lloyd under its own laws, the court held that the decisions of municipal courts and national statutes contrary to the law of nations were not applicable to the case; that the position of the Court of Claims was no different from that of an arbitral tribunal chosen by agreement to decide the questions involved upon the principles of the law of nations.   The court awarded the plaintiff damages in the sum of $446,826, with interest.[2]

The Court of Claims was established in 1855 "for the investigation of claims against the United States," [3] but it was later prohibited from entertaining any claim "growing out of or dependent on any treaty stipulation entered into with foreign nations." [4]   By Act of 1885 the court was authorized to hear and report to Congress upon the claims of American citizens against France for spoliations of American commerce during the French Revolutionary Wars.   These private claims had been surrendered by the Government of the United States in consideration of the abandonment by France of her claim against the United States for its failure to live up to the terms of the Treaty of Alliance of 1778.   The Act of Congress of 1885 was an admission that the Government of the United States in surrendering the claims of its citizens for the national interest had subrogated itself to the liability of the French Government for the payment of damages to the aggrieved American citizens.   Accordingly, in deciding these cases, the Court of Claims assumed the jurisdiction of an international tribunal, and rendered its findings in accordance with the principles of international law.   The Government of the United States resisted the cases in the Court of Claims as vigorously as the French Government could have done before an arbitral tribunal, and the ably considered opinions of the court constitute an exhaustive exposition of the law of naval capture.[5]

---

[1] The general settlement between Holland and the United States for the requisition of the Dutch vessels is stated by George G. Wilson in an article in the *Am. Jour. Int. Law*, Vol. 24 (1930), p. 694.
[2] Royal Holland Lloyd *v.* United States (1931), 73 C. Cls. 722; *Am. Jour. Int. Law*, Vol. 26 (1932), p. 399.
[3] 10 U. S. Stats. at Large, 612.   [4] 12 U. S. Stats. at Large, 767.
[5] For a full discussion of the French Spoliation Claims, see articles by George A. King in *Am. Jour. Int. Law*, Vol. 6 (1912).   The cases on international law decided by the Court of Claims are listed in an address by Stanton J. Peele, Chief Judge of the Court, in *Proceedings of the American Society of International Law*, 1909, p. 188.

In the exercise of the jurisdiction conferred upon it to decide cases arising between the states of the American Union, the Supreme Court has rendered nearly one hundred judgments based upon the principles of law applicable to the decision of cases between independent nations. Disputes falling within the sphere of sovereignty reserved to the states by the Federal Constitution are referable for final decision to the Supreme Court, which, in adjudicating them, applies the same law that an international tribunal would apply in the settlement of a dispute between two separate nations. The questions principally in dispute relate to boundaries, jurisdiction, and riparian rights.[1]

The same appears to be true with regard to the jurisdiction of the Federal Tribunal of Switzerland in the settlement of disputes between the cantons. While the cantons can enter into agreements with foreign countries only through the intervention of the Federal Council, in their mutual relations they are competent to make contracts on all matters coming within the powers of other states. "The rights and duties arising through these contracts are to be classed according to international law, and the Federal Tribunal . . . has repeatedly proclaimed that the relations of the cantons among themselves are to be judged by the fundamental principles of the law of nations in so far as no Federal decrees are opposed to it."[2] The same theory seemed also to be applicable to the settlement of controversies between the states of the German Reich. In a dispute between Württemberg and Prussia, on the one hand, and Baden, on the other, concerning riparian rights on the Danube River, the *Staatsgerichtshof* decided in June, 1927, that "in so far as the states can act as independent states . . . their legal relations are governed by the law of nations, *i. e.*, by the generally recognized rules of international law which, according to Article 4 of the Constitution, form part of German federal law."[3]

Sufficient indication has thus been given of the jurisdiction in matters of international law exercised by the highest courts of federal states, and we now return to the limitations upon national courts in the administration of the law of nations between completely independent states.

It seems unnecessary to reiterate that the conduct of international relations is vested in the executive department of government, and that when a question comes before a national court which depends for its solution upon the determination of a fact in the international relations of that government, the court is bound to follow whatever

---

[1] *Judicial Settlement of Controversies between States of the American Union* (1918), collected by James Brown Scott, 2 vols.; *Analysis* (1919), J. B. Scott.

[2] Max Huber, "The Intercantonal Law of Switzerland," *Am. Jour. Int. Law*, Vol. 3 (1909), p. 62.

[3] Cited from Ruth D. Masters, *International Law in National Courts* (1932).

determination may have been made of that question by the political department of its government. "Who is the sovereign, *de jure* or *de facto*, of a territory is not a judicial, but a political question, the determination of which by the legislative and executive departments of any government conclusively binds the judges, as well as all other officers, citizens and subjects of that government." Such was the holding of the Supreme Court of the United States in a case involving the jurisdiction of a Federal court to punish a crime committed on a guano island annexed to American jurisdiction by a proclamation of the President under authority of an Act of Congress.[1] The same attitude was taken by the court in allowing recovery upon a policy of insurance in the case of an American vessel seized by the Government of Buenos Aires while fishing off the Falkland Islands: "When the executive branch of the government, which is charged with the foreign relations of the United States shall, in its correspondence with a foreign nation, assume a fact in regard to the sovereignty of any island or country, it is conclusive on the judicial department." [2]

The title to property sought to be established in national courts, may depend upon the recognition or non-recognition by the political department of that government of a foreign state or government.   This was demonstrated in both its aspects in a comparatively recent case in the English courts, involving the legality of a decree of the Soviet Government confiscating the property of a Russian company.   The property was later sold in England by a Soviet agency there, and was afterwards identified by an English shareholder in the former Russian company.   In a suit to recover the property, the English court held that since the Soviet Government had not been recognized by the British Government, the Soviet decree of confiscation could not be recognized as valid by the English court, and accordingly gave judgment for the plaintiff.   The case was appealed, but before the appeal was heard the Soviet Government was recognized *de facto* by Great Britain, and the Court of Appeal, holding that this recognition was retroactive in effect, reversed the decision of the lower court and gave judgment for defendant.   "The government of this country having recognized the Soviet Government as the government really in possession of the powers of sovereignty in Russia, the acts of that government must be treated by the courts of this country with all the respect due to the acts of a duly recognized foreign sovereign state." [3]   In a previous case involving a somewhat similar question, the Supreme Court of the United States had pointed out that the re-

---

[1] Jones *v.* United States, 137 U. S. 202.

[2] Williams *v.* The Suffolk Insurance Co., 13 Peters, 415.

[3] Luther *v.* Sagor & Co. [1921], 3 K. B. 532; Hudson, *Cases on International Law* (1936), p. 144; Scott, *Cases on International Law* (1922), p. 61.

dress of grievances by reason of such acts of a foreign government "must be obtained through the means open to be availed of by sovereign powers, as between themselves." [1]

Although the highest tribunals of federal states may have jurisdiction to decide disputes between their constituent members as to boundaries, yet a national court is not competent to pass independent judgment in a matter involving the political boundary of the nation. As was said by the Supreme Court of the United States in a case involving private title to land in West Florida which had been in dispute between Spain and the United States but which had then been annexed by the latter under authority of the Congress, "in a controversy between two nations concerning the national boundary, it is scarcely possible that the courts of either should refuse to abide by the measures adopted by its own government. There being no common tribunal to decide between them, each determines for itself on its own rights." [2]

Another pronouncement of the same court contains at one and the same time the fullest statement of the jurisdiction of a national court to adjudge cases of international law as well as the limits of its competence in such matters. "International law, in its widest and most comprehensive sense . . . is part of our law, and must be ascertained and administered by the courts of justice as often as such questions are presented in litigation between man and man, duly submitted to their determination." [3] That is to say, national courts as such are not competent to decide controversies between independent states, but their jurisdiction is limited to deciding questions of private right between individuals. Such statements of the law applicable between independent states as national courts may find it necessary to make in deciding cases brought before them by private individuals become a part of the jurisprudence of that state, but have no force *ex proprio vigore* beyond the limits of that state's jurisdiction. Their juridical effect in contributing to the law of nations is the same as other national acts which evidence a state's attitude or practice in a matter of international relations. By reason, however, of the circumstances under which judicial decisions are rendered, that is, after impartial inquiry into all the facts of the dispute, careful consideration of the arguments

[1] Underhill *v.* Hernandez (1897), 168 U. S. 250; Fenwick, *Cases on International Law* (1935), p. 93; Hudson, *Cases on International Law* (1936), p. 696; Scott, *Cases on International Law* (1922), p. 10, note. For discussion of recognition cases in English and American courts, see E. D. Dickinson, "Recent Recognition Cases," *Am. Jour. Int. Law.* Vol. 19 (1925), p. 263, "Recognition Cases, 1925–1930," *ibid.*, Vol. 25 (1931), p. 214, and "The Case of Salimoff and Co.," *ibid.*, Vol. 27 (1933), p. 743, and E. M. Borchard, "The Unrecognized Government in American Courts," *ibid.*, Vol. 26 (1932), p. 261.

[2] Foster *v.* Neilson (1829), 2 Peters, 253; Dickinson, *Cases on the Law of Nations* (1929), p. 1057; Scott, *Cases on International Law* (1922), p. 429.

[3] Hilton *v.* Guyot (1895), 159 U. S. 113; Fenwick, *Cases on International Law* (1935), p. 422; Hudson, *Cases on International Law* (1936), p. 985.

on both sides, and the pronouncement of judgment based upon legal reasoning, such decisions are entitled to receive, and often are given greater respect as better evidencing the rules of international law than the acts or decrees of the executive and legislative branches of the government which must and naturally do reflect the safeguarding of the national interests entrusted to them.

Bearing in mind the foregoing observations upon the actual place of the decisions of national courts in the system of international law, it has been truly said that "there is hardly a branch of international law which has not received judicial treatment at the hands of municipal tribunals."[1] Owing to the introduction less than half a century ago into Anglo-Saxon countries of the method of teaching international law from the cases decided in their courts, and the preparation of "case-books" containing collections of such decisions for the use of students, the English and American decisions are more generally known, and, therefore, more often referred to in discussing the sources of international law. But outside of the particular weight they may have in cases arising between Anglo-Saxon countries, they are, of course, not entitled to exert in the field of general international law any greater influence than the opinions of the national courts of other countries, all of which should be equally judged upon their inherent merits as products of sound judicial reasoning from the standpoint of principles of international justice.

The best place in which to find the decisions of national courts is, of course, the official reports published by the courts themselves; but these are not always available. Journals of international law reproduce in some cases the actual texts of judicial decisions involving questions of international law, and in others digests or doctrinal comments are made.[2] But only an insignificant part of the whole body of such material can be made accessible in this form.

[1] See the article by Dr. H. Lauterpacht "Decisions of Municipal Courts as a Source of International Law," *British Year Book of International Law* (1929), p. 65.

[2] The leading reviews and journals of international law published in the principal modern languages are here listed in chronological order:

Revue de droit international et de législation comparée, Brussels.   Founded in 1869.   63 vols. of four numbers each published to date.

Journal du droit international, Paris.   Founded in 1874.   63 vols. of six numbers each published to date.

Zeitschrift für internationales Recht, Berlin.   Founded in 1890.   51 vols., appearing at irregular intervals, published to date.

Revue générale de droit international public, Paris.   Founded in 1894.   Bimonthly.   43 vols. published to date.

Japanese Journal of International Law and Diplomacy, Tokio.   Founded in 1901.   35 vols. of ten numbers each published to date.

Rivista di diritto internazionale, Rome.   Founded in 1906.   Quarterly.   28 vols. published to date.

Zeitschrift für Völkerrecht, Kiel.   Founded in 1906.   Quarterly.   20 vols. published to date.

American Journal of International Law, Washington.   Founded in 1907.   30 vols. of four numbers each published to date.

Since the World War efforts have been started in several countries to improve the documentation of this source of international law. In Berlin the *Institut für Auslandisches Öffentliches Recht und Völkerrecht* has begun the publication of the *Fontes Juris Gentium* under the direction of Professor Viktor Bruns, of which several large volumes have already appeared. One of these volumes is devoted to the decisions of the German Supreme Court relating to international law during the fifty years from 1879 to 1929. It contains digests of 412 such decisions. Subsequent volumes are intended to cover the decisions of the highest courts of other nations.[1]

In England there has been undertaken an *Annual Digest of Public International Law Cases* covering the entire world. Five volumes have already appeared in this series covering the years 1919 to 1930. They contain digests of decisions of the courts of practically all countries where modern judicial systems are in operation, and the cases number well over a thousand.[2]

Concerning the extent of decisions of municipal courts affecting international law, Dr. H. Lauterpacht, one of the editors of the *Annual Digest*, has made a convenient summary the scope of which can be appreciated only by quotation:

Their judgments deal with the nature, the sources, and the subjects of international law, and with its relation to municipal law. They define the position and requirements of the state as an international person, including the problem of the beginning of its existence as such, and of its continuity in face of territorial changes. They define the legal status of various types of composite states and their state members, of protectorates and other semi-sovereign states, of mandates, of other territories or parts of territories under joint or international control or supervision, of the Holy See before 1929. They are the chief source of judicial authority on the nature, the conditions, and the effects of recognition of states, governments, and belligerency as well as on questions of state succession and succession of governments, not only in regard to private rights in their different aspects, but also on such matters as succession in obligations laid down in

---

Zeitschrift für öffentliches Recht, Vienna. Founded in 1920. 16 vols. of five numbers each published to date.

Revista de derecho internacional, Habana. Founded in 1922. 30 semi-annual vols. of two numbers each published to date.

Revue de droit international, de sciences diplomatiques et politiques, Geneva. Founded in 1923. 14 vols. of four numbers each published to date.

Revue internationale de la théorie du droit, Brünn. Founded in 1926. 10 vols. of four numbers each published to date.

Revue de droit international, Paris. Founded in 1927. Quarterly. 17 vols. published to date.

Nordisk Tidsskrift for International Ret. Acta Scandinavica juris gentium, Copenhagen. Founded in 1930. 7 vols. of four numbers each published to date.

Revue critique de droit international, Paris. Originally founded as the *Revue de droit international privé* in 1905. Name changed to its present title in 1935. Quarterly.

Revue internationale française du droit des gens, Paris. Founded 1936. Quarterly.

[1] *Fontes Juris Gentium*, edited by Viktor Bruns, Berlin: Carl Heymanns.

[2] *Annual Digest of Public International Law Cases*. London: Longmans, Green & Co. Boston: World Peace Foundation.

treaties. Matters of jurisdiction, or rather, of restrictions upon the jurisdiction of the state, are their own peculiar province, and through it they decide a large number of questions of international law. Under this heading is the wide field of diplomatic immunities with its vast variety of detail, including the question of the diplomatic immunities enjoyed by persons other than diplomatic envoys proper—for instance, by state representatives permanently accredited to the League of Nations. The extent of jurisdictional immunities of foreign states, their heads, and their property, including their public ships and armed forces, belongs to the same group. In a variety of ways municipal courts illustrate both the working and the implications of the régime of capitulations . . . . and the question of jurisdiction over foreigners for crimes committed abroad. Here also belong questions of jurisdiction over foreign ships in ports, in territorial waters, at the maritime frontier, and on the high seas. It is mainly, although by no means exclusively, through the medium of jurisdiction that questions as to the extent of state territory in respect of the breadth of the maritime belt and of bays are dealt with by municipal courts. They have been frequently called to decide upon problems of acquisition of territorial sovereignty through accretion, accession, discovery, prescription, and conquest, or of restrictions upon it through servitudes or occupation in time of peace. Of the positive aspects of jurisdiction the question of recognition of acts of recognized states and governments, including the question of extraterritorial effect of such acts, has been responsible for a considerable wealth of judicial precedent. The various aspects of questions of nationality, like naturalization, double nationality, denationalization and statelessness, constitute another wide field of application of international law. So do questions of extradition. That aspect of state responsibility which is connected with the duty of the state to prevent within its jurisdiction certain acts injurious to foreign countries is well represented in decisions of municipal courts. The recent enlargement of the sphere of international protection of the individual through the minorities treaties has already brought forth a number of decisions forming a distinct contribution to this part of the law. In the domain of treaties, municipal courts are constantly called upon to pronounce not only in regard to the operation of treaties in the municipal sphere and to the necessity of internal legislation, but also on the nature of treaties, the treaty-making power, their effect upon third parties, their termination and interpretation. Questions of law connected with the judicial settlement of international disputes lie naturally outside their scope, but even here we shall find decisions on such matters as the effect of an arbitral award. There are decisions of municipal courts on certain effects of measures of redress short of war, and . . . in fields of the law of war the contributions of municipal courts cannot be ignored. It is sufficient to mention such questions as those of the beginning and termination of war, of the effects of outbreak of war upon treaties, upon contracts with enemy persons, and upon the personal status and property of enemy persons. The numerous decisions of national courts on questions connected with the occupation of enemy territory afford another instructive example.[1]

Before concluding this discussion of international law in national courts we should not overlook certain theories which have been advanced to support the competence of a court created within and for a national jurisdiction to apply rules and principles of law the source and authority of which extend beyond national boundaries. Oppenheim

[1] Lauterpacht, *loc. cit.*, pp. 68–71.

sought to explain the seeming paradox by holding that "all rights which might necessarily have to be granted to an individual human being according to the law of nations are not international rights, but rights granted by municipal law in accordance with the duty imposed upon the respective states by international law." The same is true, he contended, of any international duties which might be imposed on the individual.[1]

On the continent of Europe the problem has been treated by publicists in their usual doctrinaire fashion. Those who follow Oppenheim have become known as the "dualist school" because they maintain the existence of two separate systems, one of national and the other of international law, the principles of the latter being applicable in the tribunals of the former only upon the theory of incorporation.[2] The opposing school has been called "monist" because its partisans contend that there is but a single system of law in the world, of which international law and municipal law are parts, the former being superior. Inferences drawn from the two theories lead to different results as to supremacy when they come into conflict in the national forum.[3] To follow either theory to its logical conclusion would seem to result in the absorption of the other.

In the actual administration of international law, municipal courts have not troubled themselves with theoretical questions as to the source and nature of their authority. As shown by extracts already quoted, Anglo-American courts have assumed that the jurisdiction was properly exercisable on the ground that international law is part of the law of the land. Precisely by what method international law became a part of the law of the land is not disclosed in these decisions. Perhaps the courts of other countries which have incorporated such a statement regarding international law in their fundamental law proceed upon a like assumption. An examination of the decisions of some European courts to ascertain the theory upon which they apply international law has produced similar negative results. In her valuable study of the enforcement of international law in German, Swiss, French, and Belgian courts, Dr. Ruth D. Masters finds that "the two chief difficulties in seeking to state accurately in what manner and to what degree the courts of these four countries enforce international law are, first, that the courts rarely discuss the reasons why rules of customary international law are obligatory on them; in the majority of cases they do not seem to be conscious of the existence of an antithesis between

[1] Oppenheim, *International Law* (2d ed.), Vol. I, p. 19.
[2] See article on "Changing Concepts and the Doctrine of Incorporation," by E. D. Dickinson, *Am. Jour. Int. Law*, Vol. 26 (1932), p. 239.
[3] For summaries of the views of European writers, see H. Lauterpacht, *loc. cit.*, and Ruth D. Masters, *International Law in National Courts* (1932), pp. 12–16.

international and municipal law.   Second, the courts of all four countries are guilty of carelessness in the use of the term 'international
law.'" [1]

The concept of a single system of law in which international law
occupies a position of superiority and national law one of inferiority,
seems to revive theories of the natural law which were in vogue before
the rise of the Positive School.   We have seen from the judgments of
national courts heretofore mentioned, that in cases of conflict between
theories of natural and positive law in the actual practice of states, the
positive law prevails.   On the other hand, the concept of a positive
incorporation of international law into municipal law is too sweeping in
its pretensions, because there are important limitations upon the conduct of so-called sovereign states in their treatment of individuals
which control their actions whether they wish it or not.   These limitations were succinctly but forcibly expressed by Daniel Webster, Secretary of State of the United States, when he said: "Every nation, on
being received, at her own request, into the circle of civilized governments must understand that she not only attains rights of sovereignty
and the dignity of national character, but that she binds herself also to
the strict and faithful observance of all those principles, laws and
usages which have obtained currency among civilized states. . . .
No community can be allowed to enjoy the benefit of national character
in modern times without submitting to all the duties which that character imposes." [2]   This view was subsequently approved by Sir Henry
Sumner Maine, who said that it "does not really differ from that enter-
tained by the founders of international law, and it is practically that
submitted to, and assumed to be a sufficiently solid basis for further
inferences, by Governments and lawyers of the civilized sovereign communities of our day."   Putting the statement in another way, he
thought "it would probably be that the state which disclaims the
authority of international law places herself outside the circle of
civilized nations." [3]

INTERNATIONAL TRIBUNALS

When we come to consider the decisions of international courts as
a source of international law we are not confronted with theoretical
questions as to their competence or authority.   They are established
by express agreement of the nations in dispute, and their jurisdiction is
usually defined in precise terms; but the value of their decisions as a
source of international law depends upon the terms of submission prescribing the law or principles to be applied by the tribunal.

[1] Masters, *op. cit.*, p. 17.
[2] Wharton, *International Law Digest*, Vol. I, p. 31.
[3] *The Whewell Lectures on International Law* (2d ed.), pp. 37-8.

Until very recent years the various forms of international settlement by a tribunal jointly constituted by nations in controversy were referred to generically as arbitration.   It is only in the twentieth century that the profession has had at its disposal a documentation sufficient to begin a scientific examination of this source material.   The distinguished French authority, Louis Renault, wrote in 1904 that "up to the present time, there has been generally great ignorance on the subject of arbitration prior to the deluge, that is to say, to the arbitration of the Alabama Claims." [1]   MM. De Lapradelle and Politis, who published the first volume of their *Recueil des arbitrages internationaux* in 1905, commenced their work with the three mixed commissions established under the Jay Treaty of 1794 between the United States and Great Britain.[2]

We are now in possession of more information concerning arbitration in the ancient world, especially among the Greek city states, by the Romans among the constituent members of the Empire, later by the Pope and the Emperor, and during the Middle Ages by the members of leagues of trading towns and among the Italian cities and Swiss cantons.[3]

There is general agreement that the modern era of arbitration commenced with the Jay Treaty of 1794.   John Bassett Moore, who edited the *History and Digest of the International Arbitrations to which the United States has been a Party*, published by the United States Government in 1898, and who is now editing for the Carnegie Endowment for International Peace a collection of world-wide proportions entitled *International Adjudications: Ancient and Modern*, adopted the Jay Treaty as the dividing line between the ancient and the modern series. This division, he says, is historically correct: "After the beginning of the religious dissensions and the resulting armed struggles that culminated in the Thirty Years' War, and through the great dynastic, territorial and commercial contests which characterized the seventeenth and eighteenth centuries, there was little opportunity for arbitration. The process fell into disuse, and remained in a state of suspended animation, until it was revived by the Jay Treaty." [4]

The statistics concerning the number of arbitrations following the Jay Treaty seem to support this view of the authorities.   A compila-

[1] Preface to *Recueil des arbitrages internationaux* (1905), by De Lapradelle and Politis.   [2] *Ibid.*, Vol. I, 1798–1855.

[3] See *International Arbitration from Athens to Locarno* (1929), by Jackson H. Ralston, citing: Mérignhac, *Traité théorique et pratique de l'arbitrage international* (1895); Novacovitch, *Les compromis et les arbitrages internationaux du XII* au XV* siècle* (1905); Phillipson, *International Law and Custom of Ancient Greece and Rome* (1911); Raeder, *L'Arbitrage international chez les Hellènes* (1912); Revon, *L'Arbitrage international* (1892); Sax, *Histoire de l'arbitrage permanent;* Tod, *International Arbitration amongst the Greeks* (1913).

[4] *International Adjudications*, Vol. I, pp. x–xi.

tion made in 1904[1] contains a list of six cases of formal international arbitration in the eighteenth century following the Jay Treaty of 1794, 222 in the nineteenth century, and 21 in the first three years of the twentieth century. All of these arbitrations took place before the great impetus was given to this method of international settlement by the Hague Peace Conferences of 1899 and 1907. It has been estimated that there are now in existence between twenty and thirty thousand cases of arbitration, including individual claims before mixed commissions, from which the principles of an international jurisprudence may be deduced.

By far the greatest number of arbitrations are of claims of private nationals against foreign governments for alleged mistreatment or injustice within the territory of the latter. Modern facilities of transportation and of communication, which have made practically the entire habitable world easily accessible for business, commerce, cultural pursuits, and pleasure, are now availed of by numberless persons for travel and residence abroad, and have promoted the investment of large amounts of capital in foreign countries in the expanding international intercourse and commerce. The place of the alien in the community to which he goes, and his treatment by the local authorities, are questions which have assumed greater importance between governments corresponding to the increase in the numbers of such traveling and resident aliens and the value of their property rights abroad. According to figures collected by the International Labor Office, in 1930, there were 28,869,000 aliens in the world. They were geographically distributed as follows: Africa, 2,951,000; North America, 6,933,000; South America, 3,653,000; Asia, 8,385,000; Europe, 6,251,-000; Oceania, 696,000.[2]

Sir Robert Phillimore, writing in the middle of the nineteenth century, held that the rights accorded to aliens were based on comity and not on law. "For a want of Comity," he said, "reciprocity of treatment by the State whose subject has been injured, is, after remonstrance has been exhausted, the only legitimate remedy."[3] But this form of retaliation upon innocent foreigners or their property has been seldom practiced and is unsuited to the times.

Reference has been made, moreover, in connection with the discussion of the administration of international law by national courts, to the theory that the rights and duties of an individual in a foreign country are not international, but arise from municipal law.[4] Oppenheim supports this contention upon the positivist theory of the consent of

[1] *Proved Practicability of International Arbitration*, by W. Evans Darby (1904).
[2] *World Statistics of Aliens; a comparative study of census returns, 1910–1920–1930.* International Labor Office, *Studies and Reports*, Series O, No. 6, p. 29.
[3] *Commentaries upon International Law* (3d ed.), Vol. I, pp. 12–13.
[4] See *supra*, p. 88.

states as the foundation of international law, which, he believes, excludes it as a law of their citizens. Oppenheim had to admit, however, that the relationship between the duties of states toward foreign individuals and the protection of their rights is so close that such rights may be enforced under the rules of international law. He says, "it is evident that the several states, in order to fulfill their international obligations, are compelled to possess certain rules, and are prevented from having certain other rules as part of their municipal law." For example, every state is compelled to possess rules protecting the life and liberty of foreigners residing on its territory, and is prevented by the law of nations from refusing justice to foreign residents with regard to injuries committed on its territory to their life, liberty, and property. In case a state does possess such rules of municipal law as it is prevented from having by the law of nations, or if it does not possess such municipal rules as it is compelled to have by the law of nations, Oppenheim concedes that such a state violates an international duty.[1]

A more modern author, Professor E. M. Borchard, of Yale University, who has written a special treatise on this branch of the law,[2] divides the legal relations between states and private individuals into three categories: (1) the relation existing between the state and its citizens abroad; (2) the relation between aliens and the state of residence; and (3) the relations between the two states concerned with respect to their mutual rights and obligations. With reference to the second category, Professor Borchard maintains that:

The common consent of nations has established a certain standard of conduct by which a state must be guided in its treatment of aliens. In the absence of any central authority capable of enforcing this standard, international law has authorized the state of which the individual is a citizen to vindicate his rights by diplomatic and other methods sanctioned by international law. This right of diplomatic protection constitutes, therefore, a limitation upon the territorial jurisdiction of the country in which the alien is settled or is conducting business.

But international law does not ordinarily sanction diplomatic protection by a state of its citizen abroad until the latter has exhausted the legal or other remedies available to him in the local forum and is able to allege a denial of justice by the foreign state. Such an allegation, if sustained by the alien's government and not settled through diplomatic channels, usually is decided by arbitration.[3]

An attempt was made at the official Hague Conference for the Codification of International Law, March 13–April 12, 1930, to codify the law on the subject of responsibility of states for damages caused in their

---

[1] Oppenheim, *International Law* (2d ed.), Vol. I, pp. 27–8.
[2] E. M. Borchard, *Diplomatic Protection of Citizens Abroad* (1916), pp. v–vi.
[3] The more important arbitrations are given in Moore, *History and Digest of International Arbitrations* (1898), and De Lapradelle and Politis, *Recueil des arbitrages internationaux* (1905).

territory to the person or property of foreigners, this subject having previously been selected as "ripe" for codification by the League of Nations Committee of Experts for the Progressive Codification of International Law.[1] Agreement could not be reached, however, by the governments assembled in that conference and no convention was signed nor report rendered to the conference.[2] A collection of authorities and law on the subject was made by the Harvard Research in International Law in anticipation of the Hague Conference of 1930, and a draft convention was prepared, Article 2 of which provided that "the responsibility of a state is determined by international law or treaty, anything in its national law, in the decisions of its national courts, or in its agreements with aliens, to the contrary notwithstanding." [3]

Many of the more important claims of private citizens against foreign governments have been submitted separately to arbitration; but the great majority of such claims are referred to mixed commissions empowered to decide all cases of that character which have accumulated between two governments during a certain period of time.   The agreement to arbitrate usually stipulates the principles according to which the cases are to be adjudicated, that is, whether by the application of the rules of international law, general principles of justice or equity, or *ex æquo et bono*. Mixed commissions have disposed of many claims arising from friction between aliens and nationals occurring in the ordinary pursuits of peace time.   A late example of such a commission was the Pecuniary Claims Commission established by Great Britain and the United States in 1910.[4]

Civil wars often give rise to claims of foreigners resident in the disturbed country for injuries suffered at the hands of the contending factions, and these claims are likewise settled by mixed commissions created by the governments concerned after law and order have been reëstablished.   Claims of British subjects against the United States growing out of the American Civil War were disposed of by a mixed commission appointed under the Treaty of Washington of 1871.[5]   Following revolutionary disturbances in Venezuela, claims commissions were organized in 1903 between that government and the govern-

[1] See Bases of Discussion drawn up by the preparatory committee of the Hague Conference, League of Nations Document, C.75.M.69.1929.V.; *Am. Jour. Int. Law*, Supp., Vol. 24 (1930), pp. 46–74.

[2] For the proposals made at the conference, and the discussions had thereon, see article by Green H. Hackworth, Solicitor for the Department of State and delegate to the conference, and article by Prof. E. M. Borchard, both appearing in the *Am. Jour. Int. Law*, Vol. 24 (1930), pp. 500 and 517.

[3] The draft convention of the Harvard Research in International Law, with comment, collected authorities, and texts of related documents, were printed in the *Am. Jour. Int. Law*, Spl. Supp., Vol. 23 (1929), pp. 133–239.

[4] See agreement in *Am. Jour. Int. Law*, Supp., Vol. 5 (1911), p. 257. Decisions of the commission were printed in later numbers of the *Journal, passim*.

[5] Moore, *International Arbitrations*, Vol. I, Chap. XV.

ments, respectively, of Belgium, France, Germany, Great Britain, Italy, the Netherlands, Norway and Sweden, Mexico, Spain, and the United States.[1] Likewise, to satisfy the claims of foreigners for damages done in the series of revolutions which started in Mexico in 1911, claims commissions have been organized between Mexico and a number of other governments, including France, Germany, Italy, Great Britain, Spain, and the United States.[2]

Mixed commissions are, moreover, made use of at the end of war for the purpose of settling questions of private rights and interests of the nationals of the former belligerents affected by the war. For our purposes, it is unnecessary to refer to examples of such commissions other than the Mixed Arbitral Tribunals established by the peace treaties which ended the World War.[3]

Arbitrations of differences of grave importance affecting national rights or interests, as distinguished from the private rights or interests of which governments are merely the international representative, have been common since the Jay Treaty. They have dealt with a number of vital questions, including dynastic successions, sovereignty over islands and colonial possessions, disputed land and water boundaries, fisheries and riparian rights, cessions, territorial readjustments and frontier questions, problems of state succession and public debts, interpretation and breach of treaties, and other violations of international law.

The formulas utilized in the arbitration treaties of the twentieth century intended to exclude so-called political questions from the obligation to arbitrate have tended to create a superficial distinction between such questions and so-called justiciable questions. Many of the arbitrations which actually took place during the nineteenth century dealt with vital questions which could have been withheld from peaceful settlement by that means had these twentieth century formulas then been in force. The record of international arbitrations by *ad hoc* tribunals demonstrates that there is no distinction in the nature of justiciable and political questions; but that any question, whatever its nature, becomes justiciable *ipso facto* the moment two governments agree to arbitrate it or to submit it to some form of judicial settlement. This proposition is supported by the wide jurisdiction which the highest courts of federal unions exercise in disputes between their constituent members. For example, there can be no such thing as a dispute be-

[1] See Jackson H. Ralston, *Venezuelan Arbitrations of 1903*.

[2] The more important decisions of the commissions between Mexico and the United States, and Mexico and Great Britain, are printed in recent numbers of the *Am. Jour. Int. Law*. For bibliographical references to other commissions, see article by A. H. Feller, in *Am. Jour. Int. Law*, Vol. 27 (1933), pp. 62-79.

[3] See *Recueil des décisions des tribunaux arbitraux mixtes institués par les traités de paix* (Paris, 1921-).

tween the states of the American Union which cannot be submitted to the Supreme Court of the United States for determination on the ground that it is political and therefore not susceptible of judicial settlement.[1]

Jurisdictional objections to arbitration for the settlement of international disputes have presented themselves as the result of efforts to improve and extend the usefulness of the system by the establishment of a permanent court to take the place of the *ad hoc* tribunals customarily employed. A Permanent Court of Arbitration was established by the Peace Conference at The Hague in 1899. The panel of judges provided under the convention establishing the court was an improvement over the miscellaneous assortment of arbitrators formerly appealed to for the settlement of international controversies; but the Convention for the Peaceful Settlement of International Disputes, under which the court was established, recognized arbitration as the most equitable means of settling disputes of a legal nature only, and subsequent arbitration treaties have seldom gone beyond that model.

The Permanent Court of International Justice established at The Hague in 1920 marked a further improvement in the processes of international settlement of disputes by judicial means by providing a permanent bench of judges in continuous session; but in matters of competence the jurisdiction of the court has not been extended beyond that of the court of 1899 and 1907, except in the obligatory jurisdiction under the Optional Clause, while the matters susceptible of judicial settlement under that clause are not substantially different from the matters included in the obligation to arbitrate under bilateral treaties already in force.

It cannot be too strongly emphasized, however, that the machinery for settling international disputes is, at the present stage in the development of the international legal system, at least equal in importance to the technical and artificial definitions of judicial competence. The history of private law shows that municipal legal systems were built around procedural institutions. In this respect the Hague Courts have ushered in a significant epoch in international organization, and around them is centered much of the hope of the world for the gradual enlargement of the reign of law in the settlement of international disputes.

The cases submitted to the Permanent Court of Arbitration do not differ in their nature from those previously decided by *ad hoc* arbitral tribunals.[2] The same observation may be applied to the decisions

[1] Rhode Island *v.* Massachusetts, 12 Peters, 657, 720, 736–8.
[2] In addition to official publications of the Permanent Court of Arbitration and the Permanent Court of International Justice, reference is made to *The Hague Court Reports* (1916 and 1932) and *World Court Reports* (1934–1935), both published by the Carnegie Endowment for International Peace, reproducing, respectively, the decisions of the two courts at The Hague.

of the Permanent Court of International Justice. A recent writer who has made a comprehensive study of the law of the court says that he "has been struck with the fact that the Permanent Court of International Justice has merely continued the process of international adjudication which began to be developed during the last century."[1]

The continuity of arbitral law and the formulation of uniform rules of arbitral procedure were accelerated by the Hague Courts of 1899 and 1907. The addition, in 1920, of a single bench of judges in permanent session to hear all cases subject to its jurisdiction brought the Permanent Court of International Justice a step nearer in the approximation of international to national courts in matters of organization, and tends to promote greater unity in international jurisprudence.

Article 38 of the Statute of the Permanent Court of International Justice contains the latest and most authoritative statement of the sources of modern international law. It is accordingly textually quoted:

The Court shall apply:
1. International conventions, whether general or particular, establishing rules expressly recognized by the contesting states;
2. International custom, as evidence of a general practice accepted as law;
3. The general principles of law recognized by civilized nations;
4. Subject to the provisions of Article 59, judicial decisions and the teachings of the most highly qualified publicists of the various nations, as subsidiary means of the determination of rules of law.
This provision shall not prejudice the power of the Court to decide a case *ex æquo et bono*, if the parties agree thereto.

The first two paragraphs above quoted have already been treated at some length in these pages. An examination of the minutes of the Committee of Jurists which drafted the Statute of the Court seems to show that paragraph 3 was inserted for two reasons: first, to prevent the court from declaring a *non liquet* on the ground of an alleged absence of law applicable to a case before it, and, secondly, to avoid the danger in such cases of the judges deciding according to their personal views of right or wrong. It appears further from the same discussion that the general principles of law recognized by civilized nations may be deduced in proper cases from the general principles accepted by the nations in *foro domestico*, and examples were given, such as principles of procedure, of good faith, and *res judicata*.[2] Many other principles of private law from which analogies have been developed in international law might also be included in this enumeration.[3]

[1] *The Permanent Court of International Justice, a Treatise,* by M. O. Hudson (1934), p. viii.
[2] See *Permanent Court of International Justice, Proceedings of the Advisory Committee of Jurists,* June 16–July 24, 1920, pp. 293–338.
[3] See Lauterpacht, *Private Law Sources and Analogies of International Law* (1927).

Paragraph 4 of Article 38 of the Statute subjects judicial decisions as sources of international law to the provisions of Article 59 of the Statute. This article provides that "the decision of the court [meaning the Permanent Court of International Justice] has no binding force except between the parties and in respect of that particular case." Article 59 and the relevant opening clause of paragraph 4 of Article 38 were inserted in the Statute by the Council of the League of Nations after the Committee of Jurists had completed the draft statute. The object of the Council seems to have been twofold: to limit the operation of the common law rule of *stare decisis* in the application of law from previous judicial decisions under paragraph 4 of Article 38, and to quiet the fears of signatories of the Statute by inserting in Article 59 a provision under which they will not be bound by the law of the Permanent Court unless they expressly assent to it. Literally construed, these provisions might be thought to have the effect of reducing the court's judgments to a series of isolated statements of the law having no relation one to another. In practice, such has not turned out to be the case. Another writer who has studied the development of international law by the court says that "the arguments aiming at reducing the provision of Article 59 to its true proportions appear to be almost academic when related to the fact that the practice of the Court of constantly referring to its previous decisions has become one of the most conspicuous features of the Court's work." [1] Again, one who has devoted almost a lifetime to the establishment of a permanent court of international justice, has recently made the following comment on Article 59:

One of the advantages—if not the greatest, assuredly not the least—of a court is its continuity of judgment; for however much we may say that the individual judge or bench of judges is free to decide the case upon the facts and the individual or collective conception of the law applicable, the conscientious judge will always desire that the decision shall be regarded as just, and it is most likely to be so accepted if in accordance with a series of previous judgments which have met with public approval. Law-making is a continuous process; law-interpreting is a continuous process; law-applying is a continuous process. A judge, from the lowest to the highest court, wishes to justify his decision by precedent, and by a general principle if at hand or to be found. This is the general practice of all courts, and the decisions of the Permanent Court of International Justice should not be and cannot be an exception to the universal rule. [2]

Finally, Article 38 makes provision for decisions of the Permanent Court of International Justice *ex æquo et bono*. This paragraph was not in the draft statute formulated by the Committee of Jurists, but was added in the Assembly of the League of Nations. The meaning of the

[1] Lauterpacht, *The Development of International Law by the Permanent Court of International Justice* (1934), p. 5.
[2] James Brown Scott, Introduction to *World Court Reports* (1934), p. xiv.

Latin expression is vague and a special literature has sprung up concerning it.[1] Generally speaking, the term seems to be equivalent to the original meaning of the word *equity* when the system of equity was grafted upon the English common law from the Roman law in order to temper the application of legal principles when, according to the conscience of the chancellor, such an amelioration should be adopted. The innovation was not popular with the lawyers. They complained that equity was uncertain as it varied according to the conscience of him who was chancellor, and that the consciences of chancellors being larger or narrower, equity might just as well be measured by the length of their feet.[2] It would seem to have been the desire of the Assembly when inserting this paragraph in Article 38 to forestall objections to the submission of cases to the Permanent Court for settlement according to methods other than by the application of legal principles or reasoning. It has the appearance of an aftermath of the discussions in the Committee of Jurists over the phraseology of paragraph 3 of Article 38 which, as we have seen, excludes the idea of a decision according to individual opinions of right or wrong.

This series of lectures began with the crude customs of men in tribal relations; we had a glimpse of small parts of the ancient world; we mentioned briefly the contributions of Rome, and laid the foundations of the modern states system upon the ruins of that Empire; we have sketched the development of modern international law for the three hundred years which have elapsed from the Peace of Westphalia to the establishment of the Permanent Court of International Justice. We cannot more appropriately conclude them than by quoting the prophetic words of the late Dr. David Jayne Hill, written three years before the first Peace Conference at The Hague:

All that has yet been said or written upon this great problem probably constitutes little more than the rude scaffolding of that great temple of international justice whose dome will yet shelter the nations of the earth from the wrongs of oppression and the horrors of battle. But its foundations are laid in the moral nature of humanity; and, although—like a vast cathedral grown old with passing centuries—it is still uncompleted, we may bring our unhewn stones to lay upon its rising walls, in the faith that its invisible Builder and Maker will shape them to a place in the permanent structure.[3]

[1] See Max Habicht, *The Power of the International Judge to give a Decision ex æquo et bono* (1935).
[2] On the meaning of the word *equity* in Anglo-American jurisprudence, see article by W. C. Dennis in *Am. Jour. Int. Law*, Vol. 6 (1912), p. 614, and argument of J. Reuben Clark, Jr., before British-American Claims Commission, *ibid.*, Vol. 7 (1913), p. 687. For the view of the civil law, see decision of Vallotton, arbitrator in Norway v. United States, *ibid.*, Vol. 17 (1923), pp. 362, 382.
[3] Article on "International Justice," 6 *Yale Law Journal* (1896), p. 1.

BIBLIOGRAPHY [1]

ABDY, JOHN THOMAS, *ed.* *See* KENT.

ABREU, FELIX JOSEPH DE. Tratado jurídico-político sobre pressas de mar, y calidades que deben concurrir para hacerse legítimamente el corso. Cadiz [1746].

ACADÉMIE DIPLOMATIQUE INTERNATIONALE. Séances et travaux. Paris, 1927—.

ALBERONI, GIULIO, *cardinal.* Cardinal Alberoni's Scheme for Reducing the Turkish Empire to the Obedience of Christian Princes; and for a Partition of the Conquests. Together with a Scheme of a Perpetual Dyet for Establishing the Publick Tranquility. Translated from an authentick copy of the Italian manuscript, in the hands of the Prince de la Torella, the Sicilian Ambassador at the Court of France. London, 1736.

—— —— [Reprinted in Am. Jour. Int. Law, Vol. 7 (1913), pp. 83–107.]

—— —— *See also* VESNITCH.

American Journal of International Law. Washington, 1907—.

AMERICAN SOCIETY OF INTERNATIONAL LAW. Proceedings. Washington, 1908—.

Annuaire de l'Association Yougoslave de Droit International. 2 vols. Belgrade-Paris, 1931–1934.

Annuaire de l'Institut de Droit International. Gand, etc., 1877—. [Now published at Bruxelles.]

Annual Digest of Public International Law Cases; being a selection from the decisions of international and national courts and tribunals. London, 1932—. [5 vols. to date, covering years 1919–1930.]

ARIAS, H. "The Non-Liability of States for Damages Suffered by Foreigners in the Course of a Riot, an Insurrection, or a Civil War." Am. Jour. Int. Law, Vol. 7 (1913), pp. 724–65.

AUSTRALIAN AND NEW ZEALAND SOCIETY OF INTERNATIONAL LAW. Proceedings. Melbourne, 1935—.

BAKER, Sir G. SHERSTON, *ed.* *See* HALLECK.

BALCH, THOMAS WILLING, *tr.* *See* CRUCÉ.

BATE, JOHN PAWLEY, *tr.* *See* RACHEL; TEXTOR; VITORIA.

BELLO, ANDRÉS. Derecho internacional. Santiago de Chile, 1886. Obras completas, Tomo X.

—— Principios de derecho de gentes. Santiago de Chile, 1832.

—— Principios de derecho internacional. 3. edición, aumentada y corregida por el autor. Paris, 1873.

BELLOT, H. HALE, *tr.* *See* SAINT-PIERRE.

BENTHAM, JEREMY. Principles of International Law. [First published from the original manuscript, dated 1786–1789, in The Works of Jeremy Bentham, Edinburgh, 1843, Vol. II, p. 535.]

---

[1] This bibliography is limited to works and articles cited or mentioned generally in the text and footnotes.

BERGSON, JULES, *tr.* *See* HEFFTER.

BERNARD, MOUNTAGUE. A Historical Account of the Neutrality of Great Britain during the American Civil War. London, 1870.

BEWES, WYNDHAM A. The Romance of the Law Merchant; being an introduction to the study of international and commercial law, with some account of the commerce and fairs of the Middle Ages. London, 1923.

BISMARCK, OTTO VON. Bismarck, the Man and the Statesman; being the reflections and reminiscences of Otto Prince von Bismarck, written . . . by himself after his retirement from office. Translated under the supervision of A. J. Butler. London, 1898.

BLACKSTONE, SIR WILLIAM. Commentaries on the Laws of England. Oxford, 1765–69.

BLUNTSCHLI, JOHANN CASPAR. Das moderne Kriegsrecht der civilisirten Staten als Rechtsbuch dargestellt. Nördlingen, 1866.

——— Das moderne Völkerrecht der civilisirten Staten als Rechtsbuch dargestellt. Nördlingen, 1868.

BONFILS, HENRY. Manuel de droit international public (droit des gens), destiné aux étudiants des facultés de droit et aux aspirants aux fonctions diplomatiques et consulaires. Paris, 1894.

——— ——— 8. édition. *See* FAUCHILLE, Traité de droit international public.

BORCHARD, EDWIN M. The Diplomatic Protection of Citizens Abroad; or, The Law of International Claims. New York, 1916.

——— "'Responsibility of States' at the Hague Codification Conference." Am. Jour. Int. Law, Vol. 24 (1930), pp. 517–40.

——— "The Unrecognized Government in American Courts." Am. Jour. Int. Law, Vol. 26 (1932), pp. 261–71.

——— *See also* FIORE.

British Manual of the Laws and Usages of War on Land. *See* Land Warfare.

British Year Book of International Law. London, 1920—. [Issued under the auspices of the Royal Institute of International Affairs.]

BROWN, AMMI, *tr.* *See* SUÁREZ.

BRUNS, VIKTOR, *ed.* Fontes Juris Gentium. Berlin, 1931–32.

BRYCE, JAMES. The Holy Roman Empire. New edition, enlarged and revised throughout. London, 1921.

——— International Relations; eight lectures delivered in the United States in August, 1921. New York, 1922.

——— Studies in History and Jurisprudence. Oxford, 1901.

BYNKERSHOEK, CORNELIUS VAN. De Dominio Maris Dissertatio. A photographic reproduction of the edition of 1744, with an English translation by Ralph Van Deman Magoffin, and an introduction by James Brown Scott. New York, 1923. [Carnegie Endowment for International Peace, Classics of International Law, No. 11.]

——— De Foro Legatorum. A photographic reproduction of the edition of 1744, with an English translation by Gordon J. Laing, and an introduction by J. de Louter. Oxford. In press. [Carnegie Endowment for International Peace, Classics of International Law, No. 20.]

——— Quaestionum Juris Publici Libri Duo. A photographic reproduction of the edition of 1737, with an English translation by Tenney Frank, and an introduction by J. de Louter.   Oxford, 1930.   [Carnegie Endowment for International Peace, Classics of International Law, No. 14.]

CALVO, CARLOS.   Derecho internacional teórico y práctico de Europa y América. Paris, 1868.

——— Le droit international théorique et pratique; précédé d'un exposé historique des progrès de la science du droit des gens.   5. édition, revue et complétée par un supplément.   Paris, 1896.

CLARK, G. N.   The Seventeenth Century.   Oxford, 1929.

CLARK, J. REUBEN, Jr.   "Jurisdiction of American-British Claims Commission," (Argument before British-American Claims Commission).   Am. Jour. Int. Law, Vol. 7 (1913), p. 687–707.

Classics of International Law.   See BYNKERSHOEK, GROTIUS, PUFENDORF, RACHEL, SUÁREZ, TEXTOR, VATTEL, VICTORIA, WHEATON, WOLFF.   See also SCOTT.

COBBETT, PITT.   Cases and Opinions on International Law, and Various Points of English Law connected therewith.   3d edition.   London, 1909.

COBBETT, WILLIAM, tr.   See MARTENS, G. F. de

COLOMBOS, C. JOHN.   A Treatise on the Law of Prize.   With an introductory chapter by A. Pearce Higgins.   London, 1926.

Consolato del Mare, Il.   Venice, 1584.

CORBETT, PERCY E.   "The Consent of States and the Sources of the Law of Nations."   British Year Book of International Law, 1925, pp. 20–30.

CRUCÉ, EMERIC.   The New Cyneas of Emeric Crucé; edited, with an introduction, and translated into English from the original French text of 1623, by Thomas Willing Balch.   Philadelphia, 1909.

——— Le Nouveau Cynée; ou discours d'estat représentant les occasions et moyens d'establir une paix générale.   Paris, 1623.

DALLOZ, V. A. D.   Jurisprudence générale.   Paris.

DANA, RICHARD HENRY, ed.   See WHEATON.

DANTE, ALIGHIERI.   De Monarchia; the Oxford text edited by Dr. E. Moore, with an introduction on the political theory of Dante by W. H. V. Reade. Oxford, 1916.

——— The De Monarchia of Dante Alighieri, edited with translation and notes by Aurelia Henry.   Boston, 1904.

DARBY, WILLIAM EVANS.   "The Bohemian Project [of Georges Podebrad, King of Bohemia]."   Transactions of the Grotius Society.   Problems of the War.   London, 1919.   Vol. 4, pp. 170–9, 195–8.

——— International Tribunals.   A collection of the various schemes which have been propounded; and of instances in the nineteenth century.   4th edition.   London, 1904.

——— Proved Practicability of International Arbitration; being an outline of modern pacific settlements.   New and revised edition.   London, 1904.

DAVIS, GEN. G. B.   "The Prisoner of War."   Am. Jour. Int. Law, Vol. 7 (1913), pp. 521–45.

DEÁK (FRANCIS) and JESSUP (P. C.).   See JESSUP (P. C.) and DEÁK (Francis).

D'ECA, RAUL.   "The Codification of International Law in the Americas." World Affairs, June, 1935, pp. 94–101.

DENNIS, WILLIAM C. "The Arbitration Treaties and the Senate Amendments." Am. Jour. Int. Law, Vol. 6 (1912), p. 614–28.

DICKINSON, EDWIN D. "Changing Concepts and the Doctrine of Incorporation." Am. Jour. Int. Law, Vol. 26 (1932), pp. 239–60.

—— "Recent Recognition Cases." Am. Jour. Int. Law, Vol. 19 (1925), pp. 263–72.

—— "Recognition Cases, 1925–1930." Am. Jour. Int. Law, Vol. 25 (1931), pp. 214–37.

—— "The Case of Salimoff and Co." Am. Jour. Int. Law, Vol. 27 (1933), pp. 743–7.

—— A Selection of Cases and Other Readings on the Law of Nations; chiefly as it is interpreted and applied by British and American courts. 1st edition. New York, 1929.

DRAKE, JOSEPH H., tr. See WOLFF.

DUBOIS, PIERRE. De Recuperatione Terre Sancte; traité de politique générale. Publié d'après le manuscrit du Vatican par Ch.-V. Langlois. Paris, 1891.

—— See also KNIGHT; VESNITCH.

DUMONT, JEAN. Corps universel diplomatique du droit des gens. Amsterdam, 1726–31.

—— —— Suppléments par M. Rousset.

EDMONDS, J. E. See Land Warfare.

EVANS, LAWRENCE B. Leading Cases on International Law. 2d edition. Chicago, 1922.

FAUCHILLE, PAUL. La guerre de 1914; jurisprudence allemande en matière de prises maritimes; décisions de la Cour suprême de Berlin; recueil de décisions, suivi des textes intéressant le droit international maritime publiés par l'Allemagne pendant la guerre, par M. Paul Fauchille . . . et M. Charles de Visscher . . . avec la collaboration de M. J. Blociszewski. Paris, 1922–24.

—— La guerre de 1914; jurisprudence britannique en matière de prises maritimes. Recueil de décisions rendues par les cours britanniques et coloniales pendant la guerre . . . par Paul Fauchille . . . et Jules Basdevant . . . avec la collaboration de M. L. Léopold. Paris, 1918–27.

—— La guerre de 1914; jurisprudence en matière de prises maritimes; recueil de décisions suivi des textes intéressant le droit international maritime publiés par la France pendant la guerre. Paris, 1916–19.

—— La guerre de 1915; jurisprudence italienne en matière de prises maritimes; recueil de décisions suivi des textes intéressant le droit international maritime, publiés par l'Italie pendant la guerre, précédé d'une introduction, par M. Paul Fauchille . . . et M. Jules Basdevant . . . avec la collaboration de M. Jean Escarra. Paris, 1918–21.

—— Traité de droit international public. 8. édition, entièrement refondue, complétée et mise au courant, du Manuel de droit international public de M. Henry Bonfils. Paris, 1921–26.

FELLER, A. H. "The German-Mexican Claims Commission." Am. Jour. Int. Law, Vol. 27 (1933), pp. 62–79.

FENWICK, CHARLES G. Cases on International Law. Chicago, 1935.

—— See also VATTEL.

FIORE, PASQUALE.   Il diritto internazionale codificato e la sua sanzione giuridica; studii di Pasquale Fiore . . . seguito da un sunto storico dei più importanti trattati internazionali.   Torino, 1890.

———— ———— 5. edizione.   Torino, 1915.

———— International Law Codified and its Legal Sanction; or, The Legal Organization of the Society of States . . . by Pasquale Fiore. . . . Translated from the 5th Italian edition, with an introduction, by Edwin M. Borchard. New York, 1918.

———— Nuovo diritto internazionale pubblico.   Milano, 1865.

———— Trattato di diritto internazionale pubblico.   4. edizione.   Torino, 1904–5.

Fontes Juris Gentium.   Edited by Viktor Bruns.   Berlin, 1931–32.   [Published by the Institut für auslandisches öffentliches Recht und Völkerrecht.]

FUNCK-BRENTANO (THÉOPHILE) and SOREL (ALBERT).   Précis du droit des gens. Paris, 1877.

———— ———— 3. édition.   Paris, 1900.

GARNER, JAMES W.   Prize Law during the World War; a study of the jurisprudence of the Prize Courts, 1914–1924.   New York, 1927.

GEFFCKEN, F. HEINRICH.   See HEFFTER.

GRAY, JOHN C.   The Nature and Sources of the Law.   New York, 1909.

GREAT BRITAIN.   FOREIGN OFFICE.   British and Foreign State Papers, 1812—. London, 1832—.

———— PARLIAMENT.   Papers by Command.   London.   [British Parliamentary Papers.   Command Papers: 1st series ends with session 1868–9; [C.] series ends with session 1899; [Cd.] series ends with session 1918; [Cmd.], current series, 1919—.]

Great Jurists of the World.   Edited by Sir John Macdonell and Edward Manson, with an introduction by Van Vechten Veeder.   Boston, 1914.   [Vol. 2 of the Continental Legal History Series.]

GROTIUS, HUGO.   The Freedom of the Seas; or the Right which belongs to the Dutch to Take Part in the East Indian Trade.   Translated with a revision of the Latin text of 1633 by Ralph Van Deman Magoffin.   Edited with an introductory note by James Brown Scott.   New York, 1916. [Publication of the Carnegie Endowment for International Peace, Washington.]

———— De Jure Belli ac Pacis Libri Tres.   A photographic reproduction of the edition of 1646 (Washington, 1913); and an English translation of the text by Francis W. Kelsey, with the collaboration of Arthur E. R. Boak, Henry A. Sanders, Jesse S. Reeves, and Herbert F. Wright, with an introduction by James Brown Scott (Oxford, 1925).   [Carnegie Institution of Washington and Carnegie Endowment for International Peace, Classics of International Law, No. 3.]

———— De Jure Praedae.   [Edition of Commentary on the Law of Prize based on original manuscript (1604–5) to be included in series of Classics of International Law of the Carnegie Endowment for International Peace.]

———— Mare Liberum.   [New edition of the work published in Leyden, 1609, to be included in series of Classics of International Law of the Carnegie Endowment for International Peace.]

Grotius Annuaire international. The Hague, 1913—. [Original title, Internationaal jaarboek vor 1913, changed to present title in 1914.]

GROTIUS SOCIETY. Transactions. Problems of Peace and War. London, 1916—. [Title varies.]

HABICHT, MAX. The Power of the International Judge to give a Decision *ex æquo et bono*. London, 1935.

HACKWORTH, GREEN H. "Responsibility of States for Damages Caused in their Territory to the Persons or Property of Foreigners (The Hague Conference for the Codification of International Law)." Am. Jour. Int. Law, Vol. 24 (1930), pp. 500–16.

Hague Court Reports (The). Comprising the awards, accompanied by syllabi, the agreements for arbitration, and other documents in each case submitted to the Permanent Court of Arbitration and to Commissions of Inquiry under the provisions of the conventions of 1899 and 1907 for the pacific settlement of international disputes, edited with an introduction by James Brown Scott. [1st]–2d series. New York, 1916–32.

HALE, EDWARD EVERETT. *See* SULLY.

HALL, WILLIAM EDWARD. International Law. Oxford, 1880.

—— A Treatise on International Law. 3d edition. Oxford, 1890.

—— —— 4th edition. Oxford, 1895.

—— —— 8th edition, by A. Pearce Higgins. Oxford, 1924.

HALLAM, H. View of the State of Europe during the Middle Ages. New York, 1893.

HALLECK, HENRY W. International Law; or, Rules regulating the intercourse of states in peace and war. San Francisco, 1861.

—— —— 4th edition, thoroughly revised and in many parts rewritten, by Sir G. Sherston Baker. London, 1908.

HARCOURT, SIR WILLIAM VERNON. Letters by Historicus on Some Questions of International Law. Reprinted from "The Times" with considerable additions. London, 1863.

HARVARD RESEARCH IN INTERNATIONAL LAW. Draft conventions and comments. Supplements to Am. Jour. Int. Law, 1929, 1932, 1935.

HEFFTER, AUGUST WILHELM. Das europäische Völkerrecht der gegenwart. 2. ausgabe. Berlin, 1844.

—— Das europäische Völkerrecht der gegenwart auf den bisherigen grundlagen. 8. ausgabe bearbeitet von Dr. F. Heinrich Geffcken. Berlin, 1888.

—— Le droit international public de l'Europe. Traduit par Jules Bergson. 4. édition française, augmentée et annotée par F. Heinrich Geffcken. Paris, 1883.

HENRY, AURELIA, *tr*. *See* DANTE.

HERSHEY, AMOS S. The Essentials of International Public Law and Organization. New York, 1927.

HERTSLET, LEWIS. [Hertslet's Commercial Treaties.] A Complete Collection of the Treaties and Conventions, and Reciprocal Regulations, at present subsisting between Great Britain and Foreign Powers, and of the Laws, Decrees, and Orders in Council concerning the Same; so far as they relate to Commerce and Navigation; to the Repression and Abolition of the Slave Trade; and to the Privileges and Interests of the Subjects of the High Contracting

Parties. Compiled from authentic documents by Lewis Hertslet, Edward Hertslet, and others. London, 1840–1925. [Publication begun in 1827. Title varies. Ceased as a separate publication with Vol. 31 (1925), being incorporated with British and Foreign State Papers of the Foreign Office beginning with Vol. 116.]

HIGGINS, A. PEARCE, ed. See HALL.

HILL, DAVID JAYNE. A History of Diplomacy in the International Development of Europe. Vols. 1–3. London, 1911, 1906, 1914.

——— "International Justice." 6 Yale Law Journal, October, 1896.

HOBBES, THOMAS. De Cive. Paris, 1642.

HUBER, MAX. "The Intercantonal Law of Switzerland." Am. Jour. Int. Law, Vol. 3 (1909), pp. 62–98.

HUDSON, MANLEY O. Cases and Other Materials on International Law. 2d edition. St. Paul, Minnesota, 1936.

——— International Legislation; a collection of the texts of multipartite instruments of general interest, beginning with the Covenant of the League of Nations. 6 vols., Washington, 1931–1937. [Publication of the Carnegie Endowment for International Peace, Washington.]

——— The Permanent Court of International Justice; a Treatise. New York, 1934.

——— World Court Reports; a collection of the judgments, orders and opinions of the Permanent Court of International Justice. Washington, 1934–35. [Publication of the Carnegie Endowment for International Peace, Washington.]

HUVELIN, P. Essai historique sur le droit des marchés et des foires. Paris, 1897.

HYDE, CHARLES CHENEY. International Law Chiefly as Interpreted and Applied by the United States. Boston, 1922.

——— "Notes on Rivers and Navigation in International Law." Am. Jour. Int. Law, Vol. 4 (1910), pp. 145, 154–5.

INSTITUT DE DROIT INTERNATIONAL. Annuaires. Gand, etc., 1877—.

——— See Resolutions of the Institute of International Law.

Instructions for the Government of the Armies of the United States in the Field. General Orders No. 100, issued by the U. S. War Department. Prepared by Francis Lieber and revised by a board of officers. New York, 1863.

International Conferences of American States, 1889–1928 (The); a collection of the conventions, recommendations, resolutions, reports, and motions adopted by the first six International Conferences of the American States, and documents relative to the organization of the conferences, edited with an introduction by James Brown Scott. New York, 1931. [Publication of the Carnegie Endowment for International Peace, Washington.]

INTERNATIONAL LABOR OFFICE. World Statistics of Aliens; a comparative study of census returns, 1910–1920–1930. Geneva, 1936. Studies and Reports, Series O, No. 6.

INTERNATIONAL LAW ASSOCIATION. Reports of Conferences, 1873–1934. London.

——— AMERICAN BRANCH. Reports of Proceedings. New York, 1922—.

Japanese Journal of International Law and Diplomacy. Tokyo, 1901—.

JESSUP (PHILIP C.) and DEÁK (FRANCIS). "The Early Development of the Law of Neutral Rights." Political Science Quarterly, December, 1931, pp. 481–508.

Journal du droit international. Paris, 1874—.

KANT, IMMANUEL. Kant's Perpetual Peace. A philosophical proposal. Translated by Helen O'Brien . . . with an introduction by Jessie H. Buckland . . . London, 1927. [The Grotius Society Publications. Texts for Students of International Relations, No. 7.]

——— Zum ewigen Frieden. Ein philosophischer Entwurf. Königsberg, 1795.

KEITH, A. BERRIEDALE, ed. See WHEATON.

KELSEY, FRANCIS W., tr. See GROTIUS.

KENT, JAMES. Commentaries on American Law. New York, 1826–30.

——— Kent's Commentary on International Law, revised with notes and cases brought down to the present time. Edited by J. T. Abdy. Cambridge, 1866.

KING, GEORGE A. "The French Spoliation Claims." Am. Jour. Int. Law, Vol. 6 (1912), pp. 359, 629, 830.

KLÜBER, JEAN LOUIS. Acten des Wiener Congresses. Erlangen, 1815–35. 9 vols.

——— Droit des gens moderne de l'Europe. Stuttgart, 1819.

——— ——— Revu, annoté, et complété par M. A. Ott. 2. édition. Paris, 1874.

——— Europäisches Völkerrecht. Stuttgart, 1821.

KNIGHT, WILLIAM S. M. "A Mediaeval Pacifist—Pierre du Bois." Transactions of the Grotius Society. Problems of Peace and War. London, 1924. Vol. 9, pp. 1–16.

LADD, WILLIAM. An Essay on a Congress of Nations, for the Adjustment of International Disputes without Resort to Arms. Boston, 1840.

——— ——— [Reprinted from the original edition of 1840, with an introduction by James Brown Scott. New York, 1916. Publication of the Carnegie Endowment for International Peace, Washington.]

Land Warfare. An exposition of the laws and usages of war on land, for the guidance of officers of His Majesty's Army. By Col. J. E. Edmonds and L. Oppenheim. London [no date].

LAPRADELLE (A. DE) and POLITIS (N.). Recueil des arbitrages internationaux. Paris, 1905–24.

LAUTERPACHT, HERSH. "Decisions of Municipal Courts as a Source of International Law." British Year Book of International Law (1929), pp. 65–95.

——— The Development of International Law by the Permanent Court of International Justice. London, 1934.

——— Private Law Sources and Analogies of International Law (with special reference to international arbitration). London, 1927.

——— See also OPPENHEIM.

LEAGUE OF NATIONS. Treaty Series; publication of treaties and international engagements registered with the Secretariat of the League. London, 1920—.

——— ——— General Index, No. 1—. Nancy, 1927—.

LIEBER, FRANCIS.   *See* Instructions etc.

LORIMER, JAMES.   The Institutes of the Law of Nations; a treatise of the jural relations of separate political communities.   Edinburgh, 1883–84.

LOUTER, JAN DE.   Le droit international public positif.   Oxford, 1920.   [Publications de la Dotation Carnegie pour la Paix Internationale, Washington.]

MACDONELL (Sir JOHN) and MANSON (EDWARD).   Great Jurists of the World. Boston, 1914.   [Vol. 2 of the Continental Legal History Series.]

MADISON, JAMES.   An Examination of the British Doctrine which Subjects to Capture a Neutral Trade Not Open in Time of Peace.   [Published anonymously, Washington, 1806.]

——— The Writings of James Madison; comprising his public papers and his private correspondence, including numerous letters and documents now for the first time printed.   Edited by Gaillard Hunt.   New York, 1900–10.

MAGOFFIN, RALPH VAN DEMAN, *tr.*   *See* BYNKERSHOEK; GROTIUS.

MAINE, Sir HENRY SUMNER.   International Law; a series of lectures delivered before the University of Cambridge, 1887.   New York, 1888.

——— ——— 2d edition.   London, 1915.   [Half-title: The Whewell Lectures.]

MALLOY, WILLIAM M.   Treaties, Conventions, International Acts, Protocols and Agreements between the United States of America and Other Powers. 1776–1923.   Washington, G. P. O., 1910–23.

MARTENS, F. DE.   Traité de droit international; traduit du russe par Alfred Léo. Paris, 1883–87.

MARTENS, G. F. DE.   The Law of Nations; being the science of national law, covenants, power, etc.   Founded upon the treaties and customs of modern nations in Europe.   By G. F. von Martens.   Translated from the French by William Cobbett.   4th edition.   London, 1829.

——— Précis du droit des gens moderne de l'Europe; fondé sur les traités et l'usage.   Goettingue, 1789.

——— Recueil des principaux traités d'alliance, de paix, de trêve, de neutralité, de commerce, de limites, d'échange etc., conclus par les puissances de l'Europe tant entre elles qu'avec les puissances et états dans d'autres parties du monde depuis 1761 jusqu'à présent.   Goettingue, 1791–1801.

——— Supplément au Recueil des principaux traités. . . . Goettingue, 1802–8.

——— Recueil des traités d'alliance, de paix, de trêve . . . et plusieurs autres actes servant à la connaissance des relations étrangères des puissances et états de l'Europe . . . depuis 1761 jusqu'a présent.   2. édition.   Goettingue, 1817–1835.

——— Nouveau recueil de traités . . . depuis 1808 jusqu'à présent.   Goettingue, 1817–41.

——— Nouveaux supplémens au Recueil de traités . . . depuis 1761 jusqu'à présent, fondé par G. F. de Martens.   Goettingue, 1839–42.

——— Nouveau recueil général de traités.   Continuation du Recueil de G. F. de Martens.   Goettingue, 1843–75.

——— Nouveau recueil général de traités.   Continuation du Recueil de G. F. de Martens.   2. série.   Goettingue, 1876–1908.

——— Nouveau recueil général de traités.   Continuation du Recueil de G. F. de Martens.   3. série.   Leipzig, 1909—.   [Heinrich Triepel, *ed.*]

MARTENS, G. F. DE. Table générale du Recueil des traités de G. F. de Martens et de ses continuateurs, 1494–1874. Goettingue, 1875–76.

———— Summary of the Law of Nations; founded on the treaties and customs of the modern nations of Europe. Translated from the French by William Cobbett. Philadelphia, 1795.

MASTERS, RUTH D. International Law in National Courts; a study of the enforcement of international law in German, Swiss, French, and Belgian courts. New York, 1932.

MÉRIGNHAC, ALEXANDRE. Traité théorique et pratique de l'arbitrage international; le rôle du droit dans le fonctionnement actuel de l'institution et dans ses destinées futures. Paris, 1895.

MOORE, E., ed. See DANTE.

MOORE, FRANK GARDNER, tr. See PUFENDORF.

MOORE, JOHN BASSETT. A Digest of International Law; as embodied in diplomatic discussions, treaties and other international agreements, international awards, the decisions of municipal courts, and the writings of jurists. Washington, G. P. O., 1906.

———— History and Digest of the International Arbitrations to which the United States has been a Party; together with appendices containing the treaties relating to such arbitrations, and historical legal notes. Washington, G. P. O., 1898.

———— International Adjudications, Ancient and Modern; history and documents, together with mediatorial reports, advisory opinions, and the decisions of domestic commissions, on international claims. New York, 1929—. [Publication of the Carnegie Endowment for International Peace, Washington.]

———— "International Law: Its present and future." Am. Jour. Int. Law Vol. 1 (1907), pp. 11–12.

MYERS, DENYS P. Manual of Collections of Treaties and of Collections relating to Treaties. Cambridge, 1922.

Niemeyers Zeitschrift für internationales Recht. 1890—. [Title and place of publication vary; above title, 1915—; now published at Berlin.]

Nordisk Tidsskrift for International Ret. Acta Scandinavica Juris Gentium. København, 1930—.

NOVACOVITCH, MILETA. Les compromis et les arbitrages internationaux du XIIe au XVe siècle. Paris, 1905.

NYS, ERNEST. Le droit international; les principes, les théories, les faits. Bruxelles, 1904–6.

———— ———— Nouvelle édition. Bruxelles, 1912.

———— See also VITORIA.

O'BRIEN, HELEN, tr. See KANT.

OLDFATHER, C. H. and W. A., trs. See PUFENDORF.

OLIVART, RAMON DE DALMAN y OLIVART, Marquis de. El derecho internacional público en los últimos veinticinco años (1903–1927). Madrid, 1927. [1 vol. in two parts.]

———— Tratado y notas de derecho internacional público. Madrid, 1887–1890.

———— Tratado de derecho internacional público. 4. edición, revisada v ampliada. Madrid, 1903–4.

OPPENHEIM, LASSA.   International Law; a treatise.   London, 1905–6.

———— ———— 2d edition.   London, 1912.

———— ———— 5th edition, by H. Lauterpacht.   London, 1935—.

———— "The Science of International Law; its task and method."   Am. Jour. Int. Law, Vol. 2 (1908), pp. 313–56.

———— See Land Warfare.

Ordonnance de Louis XIV, roy de France et de Navarre.   Donnée à Fontainebleau au mois d'Aoust 1681.   Touchant la marine.   Paris, 1681.

PAN AMERICAN UNION.   Inter-American Conference for the Maintenance of Peace, Buenos Aires, December 1–23, 1936.   Report on the Proceedings of the Conference submitted to the Governing Board of the Pan American Union by the Director General.   Washington, February, 1937.   Congress and Conference Series, No. 22.

———— Inter-American Conference for the Maintenance of Peace, Buenos Aires, Argentina, December 1, 1936.   Special Handbook for the use of Delegates.   Washington, D. C., 1936.

PEELE, STANTON J.   [Address concerning cases on international law decided by the Court of Claims.   Proceedings, Am. Soc. Int. Law, 1909, p. 188.]

PENN, WILLIAM.   An Essay towards the Present and Future Peace of Europe, by the Establishment of an European Dyet, Parliament, or Estates.   [London], 1693.   2d edition, 1694.

———— ———— [Reprinted by the American Peace Society, Washington, 1912.]

———— ———— [Reprinted by the Peace Committee of the Society of Friends, London, 1936.]

PERMANENT COURT OF INTERNATIONAL JUSTICE.   Advisory Committee of Jurists.   Procès-verbaux of the Proceedings of the Committee, June 16th– July 24th, 1920.   With Annexes.   The Hague, 1920.

PHILLIMORE, Sir ROBERT.   Commentaries upon International Law.   London, 1854–57.

———— ———— 3d edition.   London, 1879–89.

———— Schemes for Maintaining General Peace.   London, 1920.   Handbooks prepared under the direction of the Historical Section of the [British] Foreign Office, No. 160.

PHILLIPS, WALTER ALISON.   The Confederation of Europe; a study of the European Alliance, 1813–1823, as an experiment in the international organization of peace.   London, 1914.

PHILLIPSON, COLEMAN.   The International Law and Custom of Ancient Greece and Rome.   London, 1911.

PISTOYE (A. DE) et DUVERDY (CH.).   Traité des prises maritimes, dans lequel on a refondu en partie le traité de Valin en l'appropriant à la législation nouvelle.   Ouvrage contenant un grand nombre de décisions inédites de l'ancien conseil des prises, et les actes émanés en 1854 des gouvernements belligérants et neutres.   Paris, 1855.

———— Paris, 1859.

PODIEBRAD, GEORGES, King of Bohemia.   See DARBY; SCHWITZKY.

POLITIS and DE LAPRADELLE.   See LAPRADELLE (A. DE) and POLITIS (N.).

POLLOCK, Sir FREDERICK.   Essays in the Law.   London, 1922.

PRADIER-FODÉRÉ, PAUL. Traité de droit international public européen et américain, suivant les progrès de la science et de la pratique contemporaines. Paris, 1885–1906.

PUFENDORF, SAMUEL. Elementorum Jurisprudentiae Universalis Libri Duo. A photographic reproduction of the edition of 1672, with an introduction by Hans Wehberg; translation of the text by William Abbott Oldfather, and translation (by Edwin H. Zeydel) of the introduction by Hans Wehberg. Oxford, 1931. [Carnegie Endowment for International Peace, Classics of International Law, No. 15.]

—— De Jure Naturae et Gentium Libri Octo. A photographic reproduction of the edition of 1688, with an introduction by Walter Simons; a translation of the text by C. H. and W. A. Oldfather, with a translation of the introduction. Oxford, 1934. [Carnegie Endowment for International Peace, Classics of International Law, No. 17.]

—— De Officio Hominis et Civis Juxta Legem Naturalem Libri Duo. A photographic reproduction of the edition of 1682, with an introduction by Walther Schücking; translation of the text by Frank Gardner Moore, with translation (by Herbert F. Wright) of the introduction by Walther Schücking. New York, 1927. [Carnegie Endowment for International Peace, Classics of International Law, No. 10.]

RACHEL, SAMUEL. De Jure Naturae et Gentium Dissertationes. Edited by Ludwig von Bar. A photographic reproduction of the edition of 1676, with an introduction by Ludwig von Bar; translation of the text by John Pawley Bate. Washington, 1916. [Carnegie Endowment for International Peace, Classics of International Law, No. 5.]

RAEDER, A. L'arbitrage international chez les Hellènes. Kristiania, 1912.

RALSTON, JACKSON H. International Arbitration, from Athens to Locarno. Stanford University, California, 1929.

—— Venezuelan Arbitrations of 1903; including protocols, personnel and rules of commissions, opinions, and summary of awards; with appendix containing Venezuelan Yellow Book of 1903, Bowen Pamphlet entitled "Venezuelan Protocols," and "Preferential Question," Hague decision, with history of recent Venezuelan revolution. Washington, G. P. O., 1904.

Recueil des arbitrages internationaux. Paris, 1905–24. Edited by A. de Lapradelle and N. Politis.

Recueil des décisions des tribunaux arbitraux mixtes, institués par les traités de paix. Paris, 1921—.

Resolutions of the Institute of International Law dealing with the Law of Nations; with an historical introduction and explanatory notes collected and translated under the supervision of and edited by James Brown Scott. New York, 1916. [Publication of the Carnegie Endowment for International Peace, Washington.]

Revista de derecho internacional. Habana, 1922—.

REVON, MICHEL. L'Arbitrage international, son passé—son présent—son avenir. Paris, 1892.

Revue critique de droit international. Paris, 1935—. [Continuation de la Revue de droit international privé, 1905–1934.]

Revue de droit international. Paris, 1927—.

Revue de droit international, de sciences diplomatiques et politiques.   Genève, 1923—.

Revue de droit international et de législation comparée.   Bruxelles, 1869—.

Revue de droit international privé.   *See* Revue critique de droit international.

Revue générale de droit international public.   Paris, 1894—.

Revue internationale de la théorie du droit.   Brünn, 1926—.

Revue internationale française du droit des gens.   Paris, 1936—.

Rivier, Alphonse.   Lehrbuch des Völkerrechts.   Stuttgart, 1889.

——— Principes du droit des gens.   Paris, 1896.

Rivista di diritto internazionale.   Rome, 1906—.

ROOT, ELIHU.   "The Declaration of the Rights and Duties of Nations adopted by the American Institute of International Law."   Am. Jour. Int. Law, Vol. 10 (1916), pp. 211–21.

——— "The Need of Popular Understanding of International Law."   Am. Jour. Int. Law, Vol. 1 (1907), pp. 1–3.

SAINT-PIERRE, CHARLES IRÉNÉE CASTEL, Abbé de.   Abrégé du projet de paix perpétuelle; inventé par le Roi Henri le Grand, aprouvé par la Reine Elisabeth, par le Roi Jaques son successeur, par les Républiques & par divers autres Potentats.   Rotterdam, 1729.

——— Projet pour rendre la paix perpétuelle en Europe.   Utrecht, 1713–1717. [Tome 3 intitulé: Projet de traité pour rendre la paix perpétuelle entre les souverains chrétiens, pour maintenir toujours le commerce libre entre les nations . . . proposé autrefois par Henry le Grand, Roy de France . . . agrée par la Reine Elisabeth, par Jaques I . . . éclairci par M. l'Abbé de St. Pierre. . . .]

——— A Project for Settling an Everlasting Peace in Europe.   First proposed by Henry IV of France and approved by Queen Elizabeth, and now discussed at large and made practicable.   London, 1714.   [Harvard College library.]

——— Selections from the second edition of the Abrégé du projet de paix perpétuelle.   By C. I. Castel de Saint-Pierre . . . 1738.   Translated by H. Hale Bellot, with an introduction by Paul Collinet.   London, 1927. [Grotius Society Publications.   Texts for students of International Relations, No. 5.]

SATOW, Sir ERNEST.   A Guide to Diplomatic Practice.   2d edition.   London, 1922.

SAX, B.   Histoire de l'arbitrage international permanent.   Paris, 1903.

SCHÜCKING, WALTHER.   Die Organisation der Welt.   Leipzig, 1909.

SCHWITZKY, ERNEST B. J. T.   Der europäische fürstenbund Georgs von Poděbrad; ein beitrag zur geschichte der Weltfriedensidee.   Marburg, 1907.

SCOTT, JAMES BROWN.   Cases on International Law; principally selected from decisions of English and American courts.   St. Paul, 1922.

——— Judicial Settlement of Controversies between States of the American Union: Cases decided in the Supreme Court of the United States.   New York, 1918.   [Publication of the Carnegie Endowment for International Peace, Washington.]

——— ——— An Analysis of Cases decided in the Supreme Court of the United States.   Oxford, 1919.   [Publication of the Carnegie Endowment for International Peace, Washington.]

SCOTT, JAMES BROWN. The Spanish Conception of International Law and of Sanctions. Washington, 1934. [Publication of the Carnegie Endowment for International Peace, Pamphlet No. 54.]

—— The Spanish Origin of International Law. Francisco de Vitoria and his Law of Nations. Oxford, 1934. [Publication of the Carnegie Endowment for International Peace; constituting an introduction to the Classics of International Law.]

—— See also Hague Court Reports.

SEVENTH INTERNATIONAL CONFERENCE OF AMERICAN STATES, MONTEVIDEO, URUGUAY, DECEMBER 3–26, 1933. Final Act, including the Conventions and Additional Protocol adopted by the Conference. [Montevideo, 1934.]

SOREL, ALBERT. L'Europe et la révolution française. Paris, 1889–1904.

—— See FUNCK-BRENTANO (THÉOPHILE) and SOREL (ALBERT).

SUÁREZ, FRANCISCO. Tractatus de Legibus ac Deo Legislatore. Photographic reproduction of the edition of 1612; translation of the text by Ammi Brown with the collaboration of Gwladys L. Williams and Henry Davis, S. J.; introduction by James Brown Scott. Oxford. In press. [Carnegie Endowment for International Peace, Classics of International Law, No. 21.]

SULLY, MAXIMILIEN DE BETHUNE, duc de. The Great Design of Henry IV, from the Memoirs of the Duke of Sully, and the United States of Europe, by Edward Everett Hale; with an introduction by Edwin D. Mead. Boston, 1909.

—— Mémoires des sages et royalles oeconomies d'estat, domestiques, politiques et militaires de Henry le Grand. . . . A Amstelredam. [1638]–62.

—— Sully's Grand Design of Henry IV. From the Memoirs of Maximilien de Béthune, duc de Sully (1559–1641). With an introduction by David Ogg. London, 1921. [Grotius Society Publications. Texts for Students of International Relations, No. 2.]

TAYLOR, HANNIS. A Treatise on International Public Law. Chicago, 1901.

TÉTOT. Répertoire des traités de paix, de commerce, d'alliance, etc., conventions et autres actes conclus entre toutes les puissances du globe, principalement depuis la paix de Westphalie jusqu'à nos jours. Table générale des recueils de Dumont, Wenck, Martens, etc. Paris, 1866–73.

TEXTOR, JOHANN WOLFGANG. Synopsis Juris Gentium. Edited by Ludwig von Bar. A photographic reproduction of the first edition (1680), with introduction by Ludwig von Bar; translation of the text by John Pawley Bate. Washington, 1916. [Carnegie Institution of Washington, Classics of International Law, No. 6.]

TOD, MARCUS NIEBUHR. International Arbitration amongst the Greeks. Oxford, 1913.

UNION JURIDIQUE INTERNATIONALE (L'). Séances et Travaux. Paris, 1920—.

UNITED STATES. DEPARTMENT OF STATE. Papers relating to the Foreign Relations of the United States, with the Annual Message of the President. Washington, G. P. O., 1862—.

—— —— Treaty Series. Washington, G. P. O., 1908—. [Series begins with No. 489. Prints issued prior to No. 489 bear no numbers; occasional reprints are given numbers.]

VALIN, RENÉ JOSUÉ.   Nouveau commentaire sur l'Ordonnance de la marine du mois d'août 1681.   Où se trouve la conférence des anciennes ordonnances, des us & coutumes de la mer, tant du royaume que des pays étrangers, & des nouveaux réglements concernans la navigation & le commerce maritime.   Avec des explications . . . et des notes historiques & critiques.   La Rochelle, 1760.

———— ———— La Rochelle, 1766.

———— ———— Nouvelle édition, revue corrigée et augmentée.   La Rochelle, 1776.

———— ———— Traité des prises, ou principes de la jurisprudence françoise concernant les prises qui se font sur mer relativement aux dispositions tant de l'Ordonnance de la Marine du mois d'août 1681, que des arrêts du Conseil, ordonnances et réglemens antérieurs et postérieurs, rendus sur ce sujet. Avec une notice de la procédure qui doit être observée à cet égard.   La Rochelle, 1763.

———— ———— *See* PISTOYE (A. DE) et DUVERDY (CH.).

VALLOTTON, JAMES.   (Arbitrator.)   Award of Tribunal of Arbitration between United States and Norway under Special Agreement of June 30, 1921.   Am. Jour. Int. Law, Vol. 17 (1923), pp. 362, 382.

VATTEL, EMERICH DE.   Le droit des gens; ou, Principes de la loi naturelle appliqués à la conduite et aux affaires des nations et des souverains.   Photographic reproduction of Books I–IV of the first edition (1758), with introduction by Albert de Lapradelle.   Translation of the text by Charles G. Fenwick, with translation (by G. D. Gregory) of the introduction by Albert de Lapradelle.   Washington, 1916.   [Carnegie Institution of Washington, Classics of International Law, No. 4.]

VERZIJL, J. H. W.   Le droit des prises de la Grande Guerre; jurisprudence de 1914 et des années suivantes en matière des prises maritimes.   Leyde, 1924.

VESNITCH, MILENKO R.   "Cardinal Alberoni: An Italian Precursor of Pacifism and International Arbitration."   Am. Jour. Int. Law, Vol. 7 (1913), pp. 51–107.

———— "Deux précurseurs français du pacifisme et de l'arbitrage international." Revue d'histoire diplomatique, Vol. 25 (1911), pp. 23–78.

VICTORIA, FRANCISCUS DE.   Relectiones: De Indis *and* De Jure Belli.   Edited, with an introduction, by Ernest Nys.   A photographic reproduction of Simon's edition (1696); translation of the text and introduction by John Pawley Bate; revised text by Herbert F. Wright.   Washington, 1917. [Carnegie Endowment for International Peace, Classics of International Law, No. 7.]

WALKER, THOMAS A.   A History of the Law of Nations.   Cambridge, 1899.

———— The Science of International Law.   London, 1893.

WENCK, FRIEDRICH AUGUST WILHELM.   Codex Juris Gentium Recentissimi, e tabulariorum exemplorumque fide dignorum monumentis compositus. Lipsiae, 1781–95.

WESTLAKE, JOHN.   International Law.   Cambridge, 1910–13.

WHARTON, FRANCIS.   A Digest of the International Law of the United States; taken from documents issued by presidents and secretaries of state, and from decisions of federal courts and opinions of attorneys-general.   2d edition. Washington, G. P. O., 1887.

WHEATON, HENRY. A Digest of the Law of Maritime Captures and Prizes. New York, 1815.

—— Elements of International Law: with a Sketch of the History of the Science. Philadelphia, 1836.

—— Elements of International Law. 3d edition, revised and corrected. Philadelphia, 1846.

—— —— 8th edition, edited, with notes, by Richard Henry Dana, Jr. Boston, 1866.

—— —— 6th English edition, revised throughout, considerably enlarged and rewritten by A. Berriedale Keith. London, 1929.

—— —— The literal reproduction of the edition of 1866, by Richard Henry Dana, Jr. Edited, with notes, by George Grafton Wilson. Oxford, 1936. [Carnegie Endowment for International Peace, Classics of International Law, No. 19.]

—— Histoire des progrès du droit des gens en Europe depuis la paix de Westphalie jusqu'au Congrès de Vienne. Leipzig, 1841. [First edition of a prize essay prepared for the Institute of France.]

—— History of the Law of Nations in Europe and America; from the earliest times to the Treaty of Washington, 1842. New York, 1845.

WILDMAN, RICHARD. Institutes of International Law. London, 1849–50.

WILSON, GEORGE G. "Taking over and Return of Dutch Vessels, 1918–1919." Am. Jour. Int. Law, Vol. 24 (1930), pp. 694–702.

—— See also WHEATON.

WOLFF, CHRISTIAN. Jus Gentium Methodo Scientifica Pertractatum. A photographic reproduction of the edition of 1764, with an introduction by Otfried Nippold; translation of the text by Joseph H. Drake, with translation (by Francis J. Hemelt) of the introduction by Otfried Nippold. Oxford, 1934. [Carnegie Endowment for International Peace, Classics of International Law, No. 13.]

WOOLSEY, THEODORE DWIGHT. Introduction to the Study of International Law. Designed as an aid in teaching and in historical studies. 6th edition revised and enlarged, by Theodore Salisbury Woolsey. New York, 1891.

World Court Reports. See HUDSON, MANLEY O.

World Statistics of Aliens. See INTERNATIONAL LABOR OFFICE.

YORK, ELIZABETH. Leagues of Nations, Ancient, Mediaeval and Modern. London, 1919.

Zeitschrift für internationales Recht. See Niemeyers Zeitschrift für internationales Recht.

Zeitschrift für öffentliches Recht. Wien und Leipzig, 1919/20—.

Zeitschrift für Völkerrecht. Breslau, 1906—. [From 1906–1913 entitled Zeitschrift für Völkerrecht und Bundesstaatsrecht. Now published at Berlin.]

INDEX

INDEX

Abdy, J. T., value of Kent's *Commentaries*, 34
Abreu, Felix Joseph de, Spanish work on prize law, 78
Aix-la-Chapelle Protocol (1818), 65
Alabama claims arbitration, 63
Alberoni, Cardinal, peace scheme, 11
Aliens: number of, 92; state responsibility for, 92
Alverstone, C. J., cited on consent of states, 50
Amalfi, Tables of, 5, 55
Ambassadors, immunities, 49, 51. *See also* Embassies
America, discovery of, 12
American Civil War claims, 94
American Institute of International Law: codification by, 72; Declaration, 48
American Revolution, 13
Anne, Statute of, 49
Annual Digest of Public International Law Cases, 87
Antelope, The (10 Wheaton, 66), 26
Arbitration, international, 91
Armaments, naval, treaties for limitation of, 70
Armies, standing, 8
Austinian theory of law, 45
Austrian Succession, War of, 14

Barcelona convention on international rivers, 66
Belgium, violation of neutrality in 1914, 28
Bello, Andrés, biographical note, 35
Bentham, Jeremy, originated term international law, 3
Bethmann-Hollweg, Th. von, German Chancellor, Statement on invasion of Belgium, 28
Bewes, Wyndham A., cited on influence of fairs, 4
Bismarck, Prince, cited on weakness of treaties, 28
Blockades, Declaration of Paris, 62
Bluntschli, Johann Caspar, biographical note, 38
Bonfils, Henry, biographical note, 42
Borchard, Edwin M., cited on diplomatic protection of aliens, 93
Boundary questions, political, 85

Boxer rebellion in China, 49
Bryce, James: cited on decline of Holy Roman Empire, 13, 15; on Roman and international law, 22
Bynkershoek, Cornelius van, 20
Byzantine diplomacy, 7

Calvo, Carlos, biographical note, 38
Cantons, Swiss, suits between, 83
Carnegie Endowment for International Peace. *See* Classics of International Law
China, Boxer rebellion in, 49
Church, The, influence of, 4, 10
Civil war claims, 94
Civitas gentium maxima, 25
Claims, private, arbitration of, 92
Classics of International Law, 17, 20, 21, 24, 25, 36
Cobbett, Pitt, quoted on custom and usage, 47
Cobbett, William, English translation of De Martens, 33
Codification, 71; Hague Conference of 1930, 72, 93; Wheaton's views, 76
Collisions at sea, 54
Colonial trade, 6
Comity of nations, 56, 92
Commerce in international law, 4, 5, 6, 76
Commercial treaties, 67
Commissions of arbitration, 94
Companies, overseas, 6
Consent of states, 1, 18–20, 24, 26, 44, 48, 50, 59, 90, 92
Consolato del Mare, 6, 76, 78
Constantinople: early diplomatic practice, 7; dogs of, 15
Consular conventions, 67
Consuls: institution of, 6; modern growth, 67
Corbett, Percy E., cited on sources, 1
Corps diplomatique, origins of, 8
Courts, international law in: arbitral tribunals, 91; international tribunals, 96; mixed commissions, 94; national courts, 80; prize courts, 76
Crucé, Emeric, *Le Nouveau Cynée*, 10
Custom: as a source, 44; distinguished from usage, 47; international legislation and, 74; objection to, 19; obligation of, 61

Dante's *De Monarchia*, 11
Danube River navigation, 66
Debts, public, state succession, 50
Declaration of London: (1871), 62; (1909), 69, 79
Declaration of Paris (1856), 61, 62, 69, 76
Denial of justice to aliens, 93
Diplomatic agents, Aix-la-Chapelle protocol, 65
Diplomatic intercourse, right of, 56
Diplomatic privileges and immunities, 49, 51
Diplomatic protection of aliens, 92
Diplomatic relations, origins of, 7
Drago doctrine, 39
Dualist theory of law, 89
Dubois, Pierre, *De Recuperatione Terre Sancte*, 10

East India Company, 6
Embassies: origin of, 7; right of, 56
Equality of states, 27
Equity jurisdiction, 99
Europe in 17th and 18th centuries, 13
Evidence of international law, 2, 51, 55
Ex æquo et bono jurisdiction, 98
Exchange *v.* M'Faddon (7 Cranch, 116), 81
Extradition, international, 56

Fairs, influence of, 4
Fauchille, Paul, biographical note, 42
Federal states, international law in suits between, 83, 96
Fiore, Pasquale, biographical note, 37
Fishing boats, immunity from capture, 57
Flad Oyen, The ([1799] 1 C. Rob. 135), 53
Fontes Juris Gentium, 87
Foreign office archives, 51
Foreign relations not subject to courts, 81, 83
Foreigners. *See* Aliens
Foster *v.* Neilson ([1829] 2 Peters, 253), 85
France, prize law of, 78
French Revolution, intervention in, 65
French spoliation claims, 82
Funck-Brentano, Théophile, biographical note, 39

Gases in war, rules for, 70
General principles of law recognized by civilized nations, 97
Germany: ambassador murdered in China, 49; suits between states of, 83; Supreme Court cases involving international law, 87; violation of Belgian neutrality, 28; *see* Holy Roman Empire
Grand Design of Henry IV, 10

Gray, John C., cited on confusion in international law, 1
Great Britain, Memo. on prize appeals to Permanent Court of International Justice, 79
Great Britain-United States: Alabama claims arbitration, 63; *Trent* affair, 50
Grotius, Hugo: common law of nations in *De Jure Belli ac Pacis*, 16, 21; preparation of *Mare Liberum*, 7

Habana, Paquete. See *Paquete Habana*
Hague Conference for Codification of International Law (1930), 72, 73, 93
Hague Conferences of 1899 and 1907, 64, 69, 70
Hall, William E.: biographical note, 39; cited on custom, 48; on U. S. neutrality policy, 52
Hallam, *The Middle Ages*, 3
Halleck, Henry W., biographical note, 37
Hanseatic League, 5, 16, 55
Harcourt, Sir William Vernon: cited on authority of text-writers, 31; on James Kent, 34
Harvard Research in International Law, 57, 73, 94
Heffter, August Wilhelm: biographical note, 36; cited on subjects of international law, 80
Henry IV, Grand Design, 10
Hertslet, Lewis, collection of commercial treaties, 67
Hill, David Jayne: cited on history of embassies and legations, 7; methods of territorial limitations, 15; temple of international justice, 99
Hilton *v.* Guyot ([1895] 159 U. S. 113), 85
Historicus: cited on authority of text-writers, 31; on James Kent, 34
Holland, Sir Thomas E., estimate of Hall's work, 40
Holy Alliance and Monroe Doctrine, 65
Holy Roman Empire: decline of, 13, 15; international law in, 3, 24
Huber, Max, intercantonal law of Switzerland, 83
Hudson, Manley O: *International Legislation* quoted, 74; quoted on continuity of international adjudications, 97
Huvelin, M., cited on influence of fairs, 4
Hyde, Charles Cheney, cited on international rivers, 66

Incorporation of international into municipal law, 89
Individuals as subjects of international law, 80, 90, 92

Institut de Droit International: report on rules of Treaty of Washington, 63; resolutions and projects, 72

International Conferences of American States: conventions on international law, 70, 72; declarations against intervention, 66

International law: applied in courts, 76; codification, 71; custom as a source, 44; dual and monist theories, 89; evidence of, 2, 51, 55; factors in growth of, 3; in Treaties of Westphalia, 54; in Treaties of Vienna, 65; Kant's objection to, 28; law of the land, 78, 85, 89; natural law as source, 15; origin of term, 3; particular and general, 53, 60, 62, 75; Roman law in, 3, 15, 20, 22, 80; rules of Treaty of Washington, 63; sanctions of, 44, 45, 46, 75; subjects of, 80, 92; text-writers, 30; treaties as a source, 59.

International law annuals, 73

International Law Association, 73

International law digests, 52

International law journals, 86

International legislation, 59, 74

International Prize Court Convention, 79

International relations not subject to courts, 81, 83

International tribunals, international law in, 90

Intervention, 64, 65

Invincible, The (44 Fed. Cas. No. 7054), 77

Italy, diplomacy originated in, 7

Ius gentium, 23, 28, 80

Ius naturale, 23, 28

Jay, John: friend of James Kent, 33; treaty of 1794 began modern arbitrations, 91

Jones *v.* United States (137 U. S. 202), 84

Judicial process, nature of, 98

Jurists, authority of, 15

Justiciable and political questions, 95

Kant, Immanuel: objection to international law, 28; project of perpetual peace, 12, 28

Kent, James: biographical note, 33; cited on authority of jurists, 31; influence of Vattel, 25; natural law, 44; tribute to Bello, 35; work of De Martens, 33

Klüber, Jean Louis, biographical note, 34

Ladd, William, *Essay on Congress of Nations,* 12

Lapradelle (A. de) and Politis (N.), work on arbitration cited, 91

Latin American republics and Monroe Doctrine, 65

Lauterpacht, H., international law in municipal courts, 86, 87

Law recognized by civilized nations, 97

Law-making treaties, 62

League of Nations proposals to codify international law, 72, 74

Legations, origins of, 7

Legislation, international, 59, 74

Lieber, Francis, *Instructions for Government of Armies,* 37, 38, 69

Liquor smuggling treaties of United States, 62

London Declaration: (1871), 62; (1909), 69, 79.

London Naval Treaty (1930), 70

Lorimer, James: biographical note, 40; cited on natural law, 20, 40

Louis XIV, prize ordinance of 1681, 78

Louter, J. de., cited on sources of international law, 1, 2

Luther *v.* Sagor & Co. ([1921] 3 K. B. 532), 84

Madison, James, classification of law-making treaties, 62

Maine, Sir Henry Sumner: cited on duties of states, 90; natural law, 26; Roman law, 4, 21

Maria, The ([1799] 1 C. Rob. 340), 77

Maritime law: authority of national decisions, 53; growth of, 5, 54, 69

Marshall, John, C. J., quoted on slave trade and equality of states, 27

Martens, Frédéric de, biographical note, 40

Martens, Georges Frédéric de: biographical note, 33; cited on particular and general international law, 60; translation by Cobbett, 33

Martin, W. A. P., translator of Wheaton, 36

Masters, Ruth D., *International Law in National Courts,* 83, 89

Mattueof Case ([1709] 88 English Reports, 598), 49

Mixed arbitration commissions, 94

Monaco *v.* Mississippi ([1934] 292 U. S. 313), 81

Monist theory of national and international law, 89

Monroe Doctrine and intervention, 65

Moore, John Bassett: cited on ancient and modern arbitrations, 91; *Digest of International Law,* 52; international legislation, 74; intervention, 65; sources of international law, 2

Municipal courts. *See* Courts

National courts. *See* Courts
Natural law, 2, 15, 44, 90
Navigation, freedom of, 65, 66
Neutral rights: *Flad Oyen* ([1799] 1 C.
    Rob. 135), 53; Piepenbrink case, 50;
    Trent affair, 49
Neutral trade, capture of, 76
Neutrality: Declaration of Paris (1856),
    62; policy of United States, 52;
    rules of Treaty of Washington
    (1871), 63; under League Covenant
    and Pact of Paris, 79
Nys, Ernest: biographical note, 42; work
    of Funck-Brentano and Sorel, 39

Oléron, maritime decisions of, 6
Olivart, Marquis de, biographical note,
    41
Oppenheim, Lassa: biographical note,
    43; cited on comity of nations, 56;
    custom and treaties, 61; Heffter, 36;
    international law in national courts,
    88; natural law, 26; particular in-
    ternational law, 61; peace plans, 12;
    Phillimore, 37; Renaissance and
    Reformation, 9; Roman law, 3; state
    responsibility for treatment of aliens,
    92; study of international law, 1;
    subjects of international law, 80;
    text-books as authorities, 30; treaties
    as international legislation, 59
Orient, The, early diplomatic practice, 7
Osnabrück, Treaty of (1648), interven-
    tion under, 64, 65

Pacta sunt servanda, 62
Pan American Conferences, 70, 72
Panama Canal Convention, 64
Papacy: early diplomatic practice, 7; in
    development of international law,
    10, 24
Paquete Habana (175 U. S. 677): cited on
    authority of jurists, 32; immunity of
    fishing boats, 57; international law
    the law of the land, 78
Paris Declaration (1856), 62, 69, 76
Paris Pact for Renunciation of War,
    neutrality under, 79
Parlement Belge (L. R. 5 Prob. Div.
    [1880]), 80
Peace: fair synonymous with, 5; natural
    state of man, 18, 21; periods in 17th
    century, 9; plans for, 10
Penn, William, peace plan of, 11
Permanent Court of Arbitration, 96
Permanent Court of International Jus-
    tice: 96; appeals from national prize
    courts, 79; Arts. 38 and 59 of Stat-
    ute, 97, 99

Persons as subjects of international law,
    80, 90, 92
Phillimore, Sir Robert: biographical note,
    37; cited on authority of jurists, 32;
    nature and object of international
    law, 29; treatment of aliens, 92;
    treaty classification, 64; work of De
    Martens, 33
Piepenbrink case, 50
Pistoye (A. de) and Duverdy (Ch.), *Traité
    de prises*, 78
Podiebrad, Georges, King of Bohemia,
    peace plan, 10
Poland, division of, 14
Political and justiciable questions, 95
Political questions not subject to courts,
    81, 83
Positive international law, 2, 20, 24, 25,
    26, 59
Pradier-Fodéré, Paul: biographical note,
    41; cited on sources of international
    law, 1
Privateering, 62, 76
Prize courts: appeals to Permanent Court
    of International Justice, 79; au-
    thority of decisions, 53; international
    law in, 76; locality of, 53, 77
Prometheus, The (2 Hongkong Law Rep.
    207), 46, 75
Public opinion as sanction of interna-
    tional law, 45. *See also* Sanctions
Pufendorf, Samuel, founder of natural
    law school, 17

Rachel, Samuel, 20
Radio in war, rules for, 70
Recognition of foreign states and gov-
    ernments, 84
Reformation, the, and international law,
    9, 15
Renaissance and international law, 9
Renault, Louis, quoted on arbitration,
    91
Rhine League, 5
Rhine River navigation, 66
Rhodian sea laws, 5, 55
Rivers, international, 65, 66
Rivier, Alphonse, biographical note, 42
Roman law and international law, 3, 15,
    20, 22, 80
Rome, early diplomatic practice, 7
Root, Elihu: cited on fundamental in-
    ternational law, 48; sanction of in-
    ternational law, 46
Royal Holland Lloyd *v.* United States
    ([1931] 73 C. Cls. 722), 81

Saint-Pierre, Abbé, Project for Perpetual
    Peace, 11

Sanctions of international law: Austinian theory, 44; Hudson quoted, 75; *The Prometheus*, 46; Root quoted, 46; Walker quoted, 45

Satow, Sir Ernest, foreign office archives, 52

Scotia, The (14 Wallace, 170), 55

Scott, James Brown: cited on discovery of America and Spanish school of international law, 13; nature of judicial process, 98

Sea law. *See* Maritime law

Slave trade, 27, 65

Sorel, Albert: biographical note, 39; cited on Europe at French Revolution, 14

South Seas Company, 6

Sovereigns, suits between, 80, 85

Sovereignty over national territory, 84

Spanish school of international law, 13

Stare decisis, Statute of Permanent Court of International Justice, 98

State documents as evidence of international law, 52

State responsibility for damages to aliens, 92

State succession, public debts, 50

States of federal unions, suits between, 83, 96

Stowell, Lord: quoted on immunity of fishing boats, 57; law of prize courts, 77; locality of prize courts, 54; publication of judgments, 77

Strong, Justice, quoted on growth of maritime law, 55

Suárez, Francisco, cited on natural law, 28

Submarines in war, rules for, 70

Suez Canal Convention, 64

Swabian League, 5

Swedish Convoy, The, 77

Swiss cantons, suits between, 83

Textor, Johann Wolfgang, 20

Text-writers, modern, 30

Thirty Years' War: armies during, 8; effect on national life, 16

Trade in growth of international law, 4–6

Trading leagues, 5

Treaties: as a source, 59; as international legislation, 74; Bismarck's opinion of, 28; general treaty structure, 64; general subjects of, 68; Kant's opinion of, 28; number of, 71; obligation of, 18, 19, 61; private international law, 68; Pufendorf's opinion of, 18, 19

Trent affair, 49

Triquet *v.* Bath ([1764] 3 Burrows, 1478), 49, 51

Unanimity rule, 59

Underhill *v.* Hernandez ([1897] 168 U. S. 250), 85

United States: attitude toward Declaration of Paris (1856), 63; Civil War claims, 94; influence on entering family of nations, 13, 30; liquor smuggling treaties, 62; neutrality policy, 52; neutrality under Pact of Paris, 79

United States Constitution, suits between states and foreign states, 81

United States Court of Claims, international cases decided by, 81

United States Supreme Court, cases between states, 81, 83, 96

United States-France-Great Britain, Piepenbrink case, 50

Usage: comity and, 56; custom distinguished, 47; evolved into custom, 57

Valin, R. J., *Commentaire sur l'Ordonnance de la Marine*, 78

Vattel, Emerich de, 25

Venezuelan revolution, international claims from, 94

Versailles Treaty (1919), international river law in, 66

Vienna, Treaties of (1815), international law in, 65

Vitoria, Francisco de, 13

Walker, Thomas A: cited on Austinian theory of law, 45; authority of text-writers, 31; *Consolato del Mare*, 6

Wambaugh, Eugene, comment on work of Fauchille, 42

War: a natural state of man, 18, 21; development of laws of, 69, 70; laws of, and natural law, 26; periods of, in 17th century, 9; questions settled by mixed commissions, 95; Thirty Years' War's effects, 8, 16

Washington Arms Conference (1922), 70

Washington, George: dedication of De Martens' work to, 33; neutrality proclamation, 52

Washington Treaty (1871), Rules of, 63

Webster, Daniel, quoted on duties of states, 90

West Indies companies, 6.

West Rand Cent. Gold Min. Co. *v.* The King (L.R.1905, 2 K. B.391), 50

Westlake, John, cited on particular international law, 53

Westphalia, Treaties of: development of international law following, 3, 14, 15; first law-making treaties, 64

Wheaton, Henry: biographical note, 35; cited on authority of text-writers, 30; codification of international law, 76; division of Poland, 14; international legislation, 74; prize ordinance of Louis XIV, 78; subjects of international law, 80; treaties as international legislation, 59; work of De Martens, 33

Wildman, Richard, cited on natural law and international law, 20

Williams v. Suffolk Ins. Co. (13 Peters, 415), 84

Windber, S.S., Piepenbrink case, 50

Wisby, maritime laws of, 6

Wolff, Christian, 24

Woolsey, Theodore Dwight, biographical note, 37

World War, prize decisions during, 79

Young Jacob and Johanna, The ([1799] 1 C. Rob. 20), 57

Zamora, The (2 Appeal Cases, 77), 78